S0-BIM-251

REFORM AND RETRIBUTION

An Illustrated History of American Prisons

John W. Roberts

S 090227

J. M. HODGES LEARNING CENTER
WHARTON COUNTY JUNIOR COLLEGE
WHARTON, TEXAS 77488

FOUNDED 1870

AMERICAN CORRECTIONAL ASSOCIATION

ACA Staff

Reginald A. Wilkinson, President

James A. Gondles, Jr., Executive Director

Gabriella M. Daley, Director, Communications and Publications

Leslie A. Maxam, Assistant Director, Communications and Publications

Alice Fins, Publications Managing Editor

Michael Kelly, Associate Editor

Mike Selby, Production Editor

Design by Morgan Graphics, Takoma Park, Maryland

Printed in the U.S.A. by United Book Press, Inc., Baltimore, Maryland

Library of Congress Cataloging-in-Publication Data

Roberts, John W. (John Walter), 1954-
    Reform and retribution: an illustrated history of American prisons / by John W. Roberts.
    p. cm.
    ISBN 1-56991-054-5
    1. Prisons–United States–History. 2. Prisons–United States–History–Pictorial works. I. Title.
HV9466.R6 1996
365'.973–DC21
96-39441   CIP

Copyright 1997 by the American Correctional Association. All rights reserved.
The reproduction, distribution, or inclusion in other publications of materials
in this book is prohibited without prior written permission from the
American Correctional Association.

ISBN 1-56991-054-5

This publication may be ordered from:

American Correctional Association
4380 Forbes Boulevard
Lanham, MD 20706-4322
1-800-222-5646

96-39441

HV
9466
.R6
1997
C.2

S 090227

Acknowledgments

Many individuals have worked diligently on this book, and I am very grateful to them. In particular, I wish to thank Alice Fins, Publications Managing Editor of the American Correctional Association; Michael Kelly, Associate Editor at ACA; and Michele Morgan, President of Morgan Graphics. My thanks as well go to Professor Norman Johnston of Beaver College, whose suggestions for a pictorial history of American prisons were passed along to me by ACA, and Richard Phillips, retired chief of communications for the Federal Bureau of Prisons, who helped interest me in writing this book, and whose discussions with me over the years have helped me gain a better understanding of corrections.

This book is in many respects a successor volume to an earlier ACA publication, *The American Prison, From the Beginning: A Pictorial History*. I am pleased to acknowledge the ACA staff members who contributed to that volume, most notably: former Executive Director Anthony P. Travisono, Diana N. Travisono, Julie N. Tucker, Barbara Hadley Olsson, Anne J. Dargis, William F. Bain, and Chrystean Horsman.

Last but not least, I am indebted to Paul W. Keve, Professor Emeritus of Virginia Commonwealth University. Paul has been a good friend for many years and has been most generous in sharing with me his enormous knowledge of prison history. Also, as one of the peer reviewers for this book, he provided many astute suggestions for improvements (the peer review was anonymous, of course, but I recognized Paul's writing style, as well as the imprint of the typewriter that he has been pounding on since the Eisenhower administration).

— J.W.R.

This book is dedicated to
Sue, Scott, and June

Contents

Preface

Nothing better illustrates the important mission of the American Correctional Association than a collection of photographs and illustrations that traces the history of prisons in the United States. *Reform and Retribution: An Illustrated History of American Prisons* is a graphic portrayal of the many methods, philosophies, designs, and tools that have been used in North America to incarcerate its law-breaking population. From its roots in Europe to the !atest technological advances, the ever-changing American and Canadian correctional systems are captured in these sometimes stark and poignant images.

With more than 330 illustrations and photographs, this book presents the fascinating, true story of corrections. Certainly, correctional practitioners and students will enjoy seeing and reading about the history of their profession. However, this book is readable and enjoyable even for those not in corrections who are looking for an interesting slice of Americana that often is neglected in other history books. This book acquaints the reader with the evolution of prisons, from colonial times in America, through the rise of the penitentiaries and reformatories, to the emphasis on rehabilitation of the offender. It also includes the work of social reformers and organizations such as the American Correctional Association and the impact they have had on corrections.

Members of the American Correctional Association often have played a significant role in the shaping of corrections. We are proud of contributing to the forward-thinking aspects of corrections, and we anticipate current ACA members likewise will shape the future of corrections.

We in the American Correctional Association promote and support the protection of the public through quality, cost-effective, and humane correction-al policies. We also provide our members with professional development opportunities to sharpen their skills, increase their knowledge, and enhance their leadership potential. By helping to shape the future of corrections through strong leadership that promotes a principle-centered criminal justice system, we demonstrate our commitment to creating a correctional environment that endorses programs and policies that recognize the inherent dignity of all human beings and that treat offenders positively.

The history of American prisons does not end with the last page of this book. It is being written every day. Great strides in corrections are made by building on what we know and moving ahead. If we meet the challenges of corrections by moving ahead and always striving for improvement, we can be proud of our efforts and be assured that future generations will build on our progress.

James A. Gondles, Jr.
ACA Executive Director

Foreword

The year was 1796; the occasion was a debate in the Virginia House of Delegates on the subject of authorizing construction of a state penitentiary; the principal speaker was an impassioned young Delegate, George Keith Taylor, who was soon to marry a sister of Chief Justice John Marshall. His eloquent remarks succeeded in rescuing a bill which was meant to carry forward Thomas Jefferson's proposal to use imprisonment as the major means of dealing with offenders in place of the severe corporal and capital punishments prevalent then. Taylor had no doubt of the reformative impact the proposed prison would have as he described what a prisoner could expect.

> *He is enclosed in a narrow cell . . . of which the walls are so thick that the echo of the loudest sounds cannot reach his ears . . . he sees no face but that of his keeper, nor does he hear the smallest whisper of the human voice . . . . During all this time he sustains the torture of having nothing to do, and his mind is compelled to brood over his past conduct and present condition. How wretched, how full of anguish must be the retrospect while memory recalls to his wounded conscience every succeeding act of abandoned villainy. Must not his mind be a sentimental hell where pangs the most exquisite rack his soul? Will he not in bitter remorse implore the pardon of Heaven and resolve on reformation of conduct? And will not then the penitentiary house be to him the school of virtue?[1]*

Here was one of many significant voices defining the correctional philosophy which was newly emerging along with other governmental reforms pursued by the new republic. With it, we have a hint of the value there can be for us in the historical account as presented in this volume. For Taylor's optimistic description of the hopeful new approach to criminal justice was just one of many such florid expressions which shaped, and helps explain, some of the institutional designs and methods portrayed here.

To study the strivings of yesterday's earnest leaders; to learn of their occasional successes, and their more frequent costly failures, brings a perspective that is humbling and instructive. Taylor, for instance, as misdirected as he now seems, was actually as "sound" in his day as we believe we are in ours. His mingling of high purpose with seemingly callous discounting of basic human needs was not just an aberration, but was an articulate expression of a theory of punishment becoming widely popular at the time. His rhetoric, so overblown in today's context, and though having a repressive, vengeful thread woven through the honest hopes of reforming prisoners, was quite in tune with the progressive thinking of his time. Today, with the advantage of a long-range overview of corrections history, we can appreciate that as harsh as Taylor's ideas now seem, they were offered as a merciful alternative to the brutal physical punishments then common. Progress, as we can see, takes many forms, and an attentive regard for the history of ideas can help us to keep our own creativity realistic.

Nudged by Taylor's passionate speech, the Virginia legislators authorized the new penitentiary, originally The Penitentiary House; construction started promptly, and the facility received its first prisoners in early 1800. Despite the high hopes that its austere, repressive regimen would be the answer to the correction of criminals, this institution, like others of its generation, proved not only ineffective in accomplishing its purpose, but even served to defeat the rehabilitative intent. It was the sort of outcome which long afterward led George Bernard Shaw to make the acerbic observation that a "prison system is a horrible accidental growth and not a deliberate human invention, and its worst features have been produced with the intention, not of making it worse, but of making it better."[2]

Indeed, history does show us some unhappy outcomes of various well-intended initiatives, but enlightened good intentions are still crucially important if genuine progress in criminal justice is to be accomplished. Regrettably, in the country's current punitive climate, it is difficult to believe that a return to regressive and previously discredited practices, such as chain gains, can be considered either well intentioned or at all useful for the control of crime.

If provocative comments like the one from Shaw have validity, we can expect a study of the history of imprisonment to give us important clues to the mistakes we should avoid, as well as the measures which may have constructive promise. Some of the early institutional experiences, as documented here, usefully demonstrate the ways in which high hopes were defeated by prison regimens that failed to allow for the human needs of prisoners. We find Pennsylvania, for instance, making the most monumental commitment to the institutional concept with its Eastern State Penitentiary, which was enormously expensive but impossible to manage in accord with the idealism of its purpose. Equally disappointing were the experiences of states that tried more economical approaches, notably Connecticut's use of an abandoned copper mine, and Maine's resort to the use of a primitive facility where prisoners were confined each night in unheated below-ground pits. Justifying these painfully crude accommodations, warden Daniel Rose faithfully echoed Virginia's viewpoint in describing his idea of suitable conditions for the prisoner.

State prisons should be so constructed that even their aspect might be terrific, and appear like what they should be, dark and comfortless abodes of guilt and wretchedness.... There [the prisoner's] vices and crimes shall be personified and appear to his frightened imagination as the contents of his dark and dismal cell. They will surround him as so many hideous spectres, and overwhelm him with horror and remorse.[3]

This concept of the necessary "terror of imprisonment" was so common and so entrenched that its long reach influenced prison architects for decades to come. These pages show the result in the pictures of frowning prison facades reminiscent of medieval castles or fortresses. And more important, the history will testify that, contrary to common misperceptions, prison life, today as well as yesterday, is not privileged nor comfortable; life in even the kindest of prisons is truly punishing.

Fortunately, these pages show the substantial changes being made in recent years toward more human penal environments even though the public is sharply divided on the proper course to pursue. Here is reflected the continuing tension in our society between people of different viewpoints regarding the purpose and nature of public punishment. Many, who speak from their anger about crime, are eager to see criminal offenders again suffering humiliating punishment in bleak and austere prisons. The prevalence and strength of such views are made evident by the steady increase in the country's prison populations.

At the same time, the more human architecture of the new prisons reflects the view of many criminal justice leaders that penal habitats must be decently considerate of human needs whether or not this will result in a better corrective effect. For they believe that it is by treating even the least popular and least deserving of its citizens with unfailing basic decency, that a great nation affirms its guarantee of maintaining the most orderly and civilized society for the benefit of everyone.

Those who advocate the more rigorously punitive prisons also tend to give very little respect to the idea of "prisoners' rights." But here again, the treatment accorded the criminal offender is a key to the treatment that every citizen may expect. In this sense, the integrity of the criminal law is vital to the protection of the rights of all citizens. Making this point in a simple way, U.S. Justice William J. Brennan remarked that ". . . it is only by upholding fundamental principles, even at the expense of freeing some not very nice people, that the protections for nice people are maintained."[4]

Another noteworthy person who spoke to this point was Winston Churchill, who took his first important post in the British government when appointed Home Secretary in 1910. While carrying this responsibility for administration of the police and correctional services of his country, Churchill declared in a speech to Parliament that:

> *The mood and temper of the public in regard to the treatment of crime and criminals is one of the most unfailing tests of any country. A calm, dispassionate recognition of the rights of the accused, and even of the convicted criminal . . . are the symbols which . . . make and measure the stored up strength of a nation, and are sign and proof of the living virtue within it.*[5]

This is a thought that deserves our respect as legislatures formulate criminal justice laws, or as planners design correctional environments. This illustrated history will be particularly valuable if it provides a clear perspective on the country's progress toward a correctional system that not only contributes effectively to everyday public safety, but which also helps preserve the basic rights that are meant for all to enjoy in a great democracy.

Paul W. Keve

NOTES

[1] Virginia State Library Archives, George Keith Taylor, *Speech Delivered to the House of Delegates on the Bill to Amend the Penal Laws of this Commonwealth.* 1796. p. 31.

[2] George Bernard Shaw, *The Crime of Imprisonment*, New York, Greenwood Press. 1946. p. 104.

[3] Daniel Rose in Teeters, Negley and John D. Shearer, *The Prison at Philadelphia, Cherry Hill: The Separate System of Penal Discipline, 1829-1913*, New York: Columbia University Press, 1957. p. 26.

[4] William J. Brennan, *American Bar Association Journal*, Vol. 49, March 1963, p. 239.

[5] Winston Churchill, from a speech in the House of Commons, July 20, 1910.

1

European Influences on American Prisons

Imprisonment as a means of punishment is a relatively modern practice. Before the eighteenth century, offenders typically were sentenced to death, mutilation, branding, flogging, or banishment to a colonial territory—but they were seldom sentenced to confinement in a prison as punishment for their crimes. Instead, prisons were used mainly to house accused persons awaiting trial, and convicts awaiting sentencing. Sometimes they also held debtors and political prisoners. Many early prisons were forts or castles adapted for that purpose, such as the Tower of London, the Bastille in Paris, and Switzerland's Chillon Castle.

Before imprisonment was adopted as a standard criminal sanction, physical torture or death was prescribed as punishment for most crimes. A garrote was an iron collar that could be locked around an offender's neck—to disable or torture the offender, or, if tightened, to strangle the offender to death.

Etching by Goya, Library of Congress

Earliest Prisons

Six thousand years ago in Babylon, the most common punishments for criminals were execution or mutilation. The Babylonians did maintain prisons, however, for petty offenders and debtors, and for convicts who happened to be slaves or foreigners.

In ancient Athens, a committee of magistrates called "The Eleven" supervised a system of prisons, although the chief punishment options included fines, exile, stoning, crucifixion, and "precipitation"—or flinging unfortunate lawbreakers off high cliffs. In 399 B.C., Socrates considered the prospect of incarceration so odious that he preferred a draft of hemlock to the clutches of "The Eleven"—albeit for philosophical motives rather than considerations of personal comfort.

Several references to prisons appear in the Bible. The Old Testament contains accounts of imprisonment imposed by the Egyptians, Philistines, Israelites, and Assyrians. The New Testament covers the imprisonment in Rome of early Christians awaiting miserable deaths in the Colosseum.

Among the places of confinement in ancient Rome were a series of dungeons known as the Mamartine Prison. Built underground in 64 B.C., the Mamartine Prison housed offenders in large, caged rooms. Later, Roman prisoners were kept in stone quarries and similar places originally created for other purposes.

From the fourth century A.D. until the Renaissance, the Roman Catholic Church contributed greatly to the evolution of the prison. Throughout Europe and in England, bishops and abbots exercised authority to imprison both clergy and laypeople who violated canon law, often in special chambers within monasteries and abbeys. Among the most notable examples of ecclesiastical prisons were those used during the Inquisition of the fourteenth and fifteenth centuries to confine religious heretics.

European monarchs used castle dungeons to imprison political opponents or individuals who coveted the throne.

unknown

The Bastille being stormed in 1789, during the French Revolution. While popular history has overestimated its significance as a political prison, the Bastille was an example of a castle that was used to confine prisoners.

Engraving by Pierre Gabriel Berthault (1798), New York Public Library

Tales of cruelty in the monastic prisons circulated widely in the eighteenth and nineteenth centuries, and there were certainly many instances of physical abuse. In the 1300s, for example, monks in Toulouse, France, protested the severe conditions in one monastic prison. The prisons operated by the Church, however, represented an important advance in the nature of imprisonment. Inmates were not confined simply to await corporal or capital punishment; the ecclesiastical prisons were an *alternative* to other forms of punishment. Because offenders were confined in order for them to do penance for their sins and attain salvation, the ecclesiastical prisons were not merely places of confinement. Instead, they aimed at reforming or correcting the offender.

Secular prisons began to emerge as early as the twelfth century, with the rise of civil governments in Europe and the development of public law. Even before then, ruling monarchs found castles to be suitable places to lock away political rivals. In England, for example, William I began using the Tower of London to imprison his enemies a few years after the Norman Conquest of 1066.

In 1166, England's Henry II ordered county sheriffs throughout his domain to build jails (or "gaols") to hold defendants awaiting trial. By the thirteenth and fourteenth centuries, prisons—usually located in castles or other fortifications—started appearing in France and in the various kingdoms and city-states of Germany and Italy.

Execution, torture on the rack or wheel, mutilation (including amputation and blinding), and loss of property remained the most prevalent forms of punishment during the late Middle Ages, and prisons continued to be used principally to house offenders until those sentences could be imposed. Nevertheless, there was a growing body of crimes—usually misdemeanors and morals offenses—for which the punishment was incarceration.

Many of the early European prisons attempted to segregate prisoners by sex, and in some instances female prisoners were guarded by female jailers. Le Stinche prison, built in the 1290s in Florence, Italy, separated prisoners not only by sex but also by age group, degree of sanity, and severity of offense. Likewise, the Maison de Force, a prison in Ghent, Belgium, and the Amsterdam House of Correction, developed classification systems to separate serious from minor offenders, and a wing of the Hospice of San Michele in Rome contained an early version of a juvenile reformatory.

Federal Bureau of Prisons, *Handbook of Correctional Institution Design and Construction* (1949)

Early European prisons held men and women, violent criminals and nonviolent debtors, and even adults and children, in common rooms; there was little or no attempt to classify or segregate them.

Typically, however, the only classification of inmates was by social standing and ability to pay for better accommodations. Jailers received little or no financial support from governments, but were entitled to collect fees from inmates for food and other necessities. Incarcerated nobles who could pay the heftiest fees lived in comparative comfort with a modicum of privacy; less affluent prisoners were confined in large common rooms; the poorest inmates, and those who were considered the most dangerous, had to endure squalid dungeons. It was not unusual for men, women, and children, the sane and the mentally ill, felons and misdemeanants, all to be crowded indiscriminately in group cells.

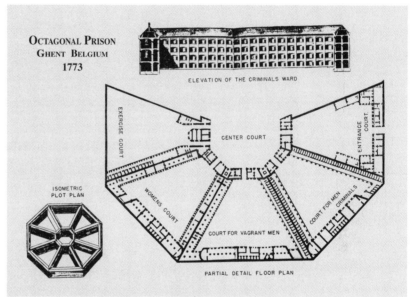

Plans for early European prisons: the prison at Ghent, Belgium (1773) and below, St. Michele in Rome (1704).

Federal Bureau of Prisons, *Handbook of Correctional Institution Design and Construction* (1949)

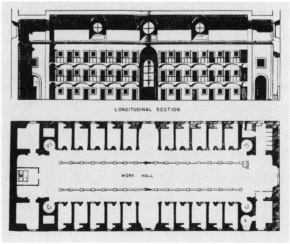

Mayhew and Binny, *Criminal Prisons of London* (1862)

Bridewells, Banishment, and Hulks

The Bridewells were named after the first workhouse—London's Bridewell Palace— an old mansion that had been converted into a workhouse in 1557.

By the fifteenth century, the breakup of feudalism and the subsequent expansion of urban areas caused severe social and economic turmoil. Workers, sometimes in groups, roamed from town to town in search of employment—an inherently unstable population that was a source of serious concern for rural landlords and urban citizens alike. Further, landless peasants and others unable to find work resorted to vagrancy, begging, and petty theft.

The English Parliament responded with laws that restricted the movement and wages of urban workers, and mandated branding, mutilation, and other forms of corporal punishment for vagrants. Those measures were as inadequate as they were brutal, and England ultimately devised a new response: prison-like workhouses called Bridewells.

The Bridewells were named after the first workhouse—London's Bridewell Palace—an old mansion that had been converted into a workhouse in 1557. Parliament soon required every county to open a Bridewell.

Vagrants, the destitute, and petty criminals were confined at Bridewells under strict discipline, often subjected to physical abuse, and required to work at such tasks as manufacturing various products, baking, and milling. While in many respects a humane advance, the Bridewells were always grim places. By the eighteenth century, they had deteriorated into truly miserable operations.

The end of feudalism also was accompanied by the Age of Exploration, the rise of mercantilism, and the settlement of overseas colonies by the European powers. Those developments, in turn, made possible a new form of criminal incarceration: the transportation or banishment of convicts to penal colonies in Africa, Australia, and the Americas, primarily during the 1700s and 1800s.

Spain confined convicts in its colonies in the Canary Islands and North Africa. Russia's great penal colony was Siberia. New Caledonia, a Pacific island west of Australia, was a French penal colony, as was French Guiana in South America—which included the notorious Devil's Island. France did not close its penal colony in French Guiana until after World War II.

Mayhew and Binny, *Criminal Prisons of London* (1862)

During the mid-nineteenth century, the workrooms for women at Tothill Fields Prison in England, and for men at Coldbath Fields Prison, resembled the workrooms in the Bridewells that had begun to appear in England in the sixteenth century.

In the seventeenth and eighteenth centuries, England transported convicts to its American colonies, where they were auctioned off to settlers as indentured servants. Following the American Revolution, England relied on Australia as a penal colony.

Australia even had a prison colony of its own—Norfolk Island—reserved for the most desperate criminals and for English criminals exiled to Australia only to commit additional crimes after they got there. The infamous brutality of Norfolk Island was relieved only by the brief but enlightened superintendentship of Captain Alexander Maconochie from 1839 to 1843. Maconochie (1787-1860) emphasized rehabilitation and compassionate treatment, dramatically reduced the use of corporal punishment, and instituted a system of releasing inmates based not on time served but on demonstration of good behavior and sound attitudes. Years later, after his death, Maconochie's ideas became enormously influential among prison administrators. Yet, he failed during his years as superintendent to persuade his superiors in London of the wisdom of his reforms, and Norfolk Island reverted to its brutal ways after he was removed from office.

K.S. Maconochie

Captain Alexander Maconochie, the visionary superintendent of Australia's Norfolk Island penal colony.

Public Library, New South Wales

One of Australia's penal colonies, located in Kingston (shown in the late 1840s).

Reform and Retribution: An Illustrated History of American Prisons

Bridewells, prisons, and transportation to colonies could not keep up with England's expanding inmate population. Starting in the mid-1700s, England turned to incarcerating some offenders in derelict warships and merchant vessels called *hulks*. Intended as a temporary expedient, the practice lasted until well into the mid-1800s. At least one hulk, anchored off the coast of Gibraltar, was still in use as late as 1875. The English also used hulks in the Hudson River to confine prisoners of war captured during the American Revolution. Actually, ships had been used for confining inmates even before the eighteenth century. For hundreds of years, up until the late 1800s, England and France had forced criminals and prisoners of war to man oars on warships known as "galleys."

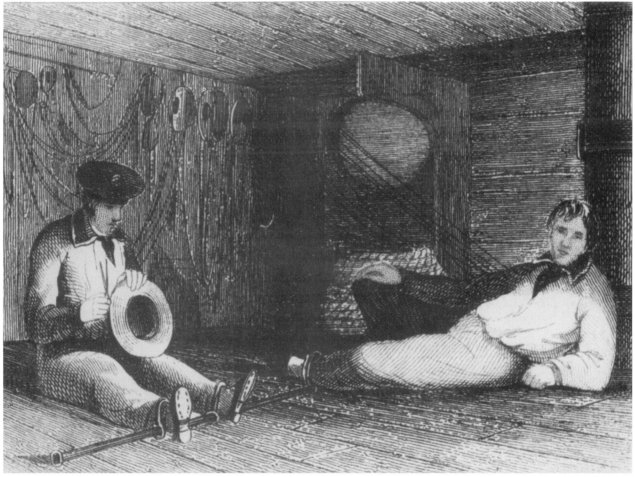

Library of Congress

Inmates in the hold of a British hulk, ca. 1800.

In the eighteenth and nineteenth centuries, British convicts were imprisoned on derelict vessels anchored mainly in the Woolwich, Portsmouth, and Deptford harbors, and also at Bermuda and Gibraltar.

Mayhew and Binny, *Criminal Prisons of London* (1862)

The British hulk, H.M.S. York

Mayhew and Binny, *Criminal Prisons of London* (1862)

Hulks were anchored in bays and rivers throughout Britain. As many as 5,000 convicts were imprisoned on hulks at any given time during the nineteenth century, although many were removed from the ships by day to perform hard labor on government projects or for private contractors. Conditions aboard the ships were horrendous. No longer seaworthy, some hulks took on so much water that there were drownings among inmates confined to lower decks. The hulks were filthy, crowded, unventilated, disease-ridden, and infested with vermin. The food was inadequate, and discipline was harsh.

Sectional view of the British prison hulk, "Defence."

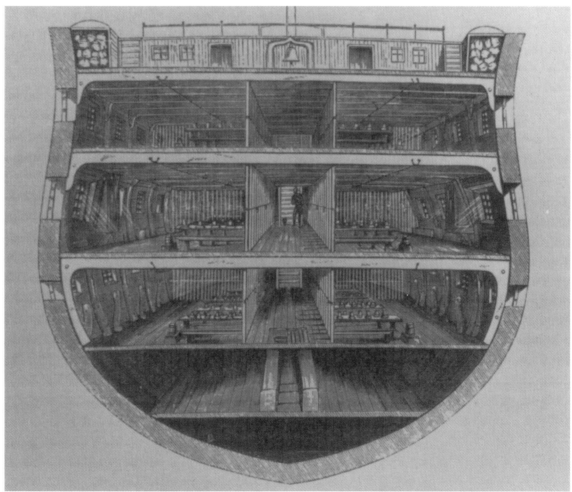

Mayhew and Binny, *Criminal Prisons of London* (1862)

Chapel services
on the "Defence."

Mayhew and Binny, *Criminal Prisons of London* (1862)

An upper deck of the
"Unite," a hulk that
served in the mid-
nineteenth century as
a hospital for inmates
from adjacent prison
hulks moored at Wool-
wich harbor in Britain.

Mayhew and Binny, *Criminal Prisons of London* (1862)

The History of the British Convict Ship "Success" and Its Most Notorious Prisoners, (1912)

A garrote, leg irons, handcuffs, and balls and chains were among the implements of restraint and torture displayed on the "Success."

The History of the British Convict Ship "Success" and Its Most Notorious Prisoners (1912)

In the 1890s and early 1900s, the "Success" was a floating museum that recreated conditions aboard the English prison hulks.

A Great Wave of Reform

The eighteenth century was the Age of Enlightenment in Western Europe. Yet, the punishments meted out to wrongdoers as the century opened were unbelievably cruel and far from enlightened. Convicts who were merely flogged were the lucky ones. It was not unusual for convicts to have limbs, ears, or lips severed as punishment. Hangings and decapitations were common punishments and often took place before delighted crowds enjoying an afternoon's entertainment. Even in death, convicts were punished. After execution, it was not unusual for criminals' bodies to be hacked apart, and the heads impaled on stakes in public places.

Incarceration in pestilent, dangerous, and overcrowded jails, workhouses, and hulks was not much better. Living conditions were deplorable; beatings were a preferred method of maintaining discipline; and many jailers were corrupt—charging outrageous fees to inmates for meager rations and miserable accommodations.

By the middle of the eighteenth century, respected philosophers and reformers in England and throughout Europe were decrying the horrors of criminal punishment. The sanctions being imposed, they argued, degraded not only the convicts being punished, but also society itself. In keeping with the intellectual currents of the day, they urged sanctions that were more rational, more enlightened, and more humane.

Mayhew and Binny, *Criminal Prisons of London* (1862)

By the mid-1800s, prison reforms were taking hold in Britain. The school for girls and the exercise yard for boys at Tothill Fields Prison were examples of improved programming, better conditions, and the separation of inmates by sex and age.

Mayhew and Binny, *Criminal Prisons of London* (1862)

"The end of punishment [is to] prevent the criminal from doing further injury to society and to prevent others from committing the like offense."

–Beccaria

Among those who spoke out against inhumane punishments were Frederick II of Prussia and the French philosophers Voltaire, Montesquieu, and Diderot. The Italian Cesare Beccaria and the Englishman Jeremy Bentham proposed more humane prisons as part of a more rational and systematic criminal justice system. Bentham proposed new designs to make prisons more secure, more easily managed, and better able to rehabilitate offenders. Beccaria called for better legal procedures in trials, impartial sentencing, and an end to torture and capital punishment. He also sought to define reason in punishment: "The purpose of punishment is not to torment a sensible being, not to undo a crime already committed," he wrote in 1764. "The end of punishment [is to] prevent the criminal from doing further injury to society and to prevent others from committing the like offense." Meanwhile, John Howard of England developed an array of internal prison reforms, including better sanitation, religious instruction to promote moral reform, and inmate labor to encourage self-discipline.

This nineteenth century British cellblock shows the influence of the architectural style developed in Auburn, New York (see Chapter 3).

Mayhew and Binny, *Criminal Prisons of London* (1862)

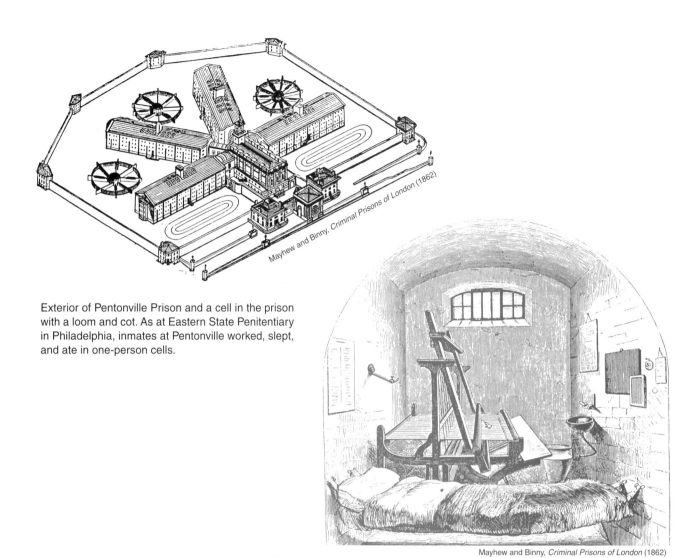

Mayhew and Binny, *Criminal Prisons of London* (1862)

Exterior of Pentonville Prison and a cell in the prison with a loom and cot. As at Eastern State Penitentiary in Philadelphia, inmates at Pentonville worked, slept, and ate in one-person cells.

Mayhew and Binny, *Criminal Prisons of London* (1862)

Reflecting the "separate system" pioneered in the United States (see Chapter 3), Pentonville Prison in Great Britain provided individual booths for inmates to attend religious services in the mid-1800s.

Bidwell, *Forging His Chains* (1889)

Reform and Retribution: An Illustrated History of American Prisons

As the reform impulse took shape, several themes emerged. First, punishment should not be brutal, excessive, or oriented toward retribution or vengeance, but should fit the crime. Second, criminal codes and punishments should be clear, rational, and equitably applied, and trials should be open to public scrutiny. Third, fixed prison terms—not open-ended sentences, not torture or execution—should be the method for punishing lawbreakers. Finally, the prisons where the lawbreakers would be confined should be clean, safe, and operated in an orderly, honest, and competent manner; they should be supported by government rather than exorbitant fees charged to the inmates; and the inmates should always be segregated by sex and by the severity of offense; sane and insane inmates should not be housed together; and youthful prisoners should be separated from adult prisoners.

The British Parliament attempted to implement some of these reforms under the Hard Labour Act (or Penitentiary Act) of 1779. Wymondham Gaol (jail) in Norfolk was erected six years later in accordance with that legislation, which mandated secure and sanitary structures and regular inspections, and prohibited the collection of fees from prisoners. In 1791, the French National Assembly authorized similar types of prisons.

Finley, *Memorial of Prison Life* (1854)

Inmates in nineteenth century British prison speak with visitors through an iron grille (left) and are fed under the curious gaping of a well-to-do observer and his children (below).

Mayhew and Binny, *Criminal Prisons of London* (1862)

The concept of prisons as humane places of confinement where offenders would be deprived of their liberty temporarily as the primary form of punishment, however, did not take hold quickly in Europe. Provincial prisons in France failed to undertake the reforms pushed by the National Assembly in Paris. There was resistance, too, in England, which for decades neglected the humane prison ideal in favor of transporting criminals to its penal colony in Australia. It remained for a new country—the United States—to give the penitentiary concept its first great test.

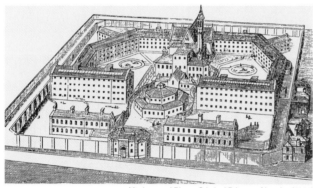

Mayhew and Binny, *Criminal Prisons of London* (1862)

Inmate classification at Brixton women's prison in Britain in the mid-nineteenth century: aerial and interior views.

Mayhew and Binny, *Criminal Prisons of London* (1862)

Inmates with their children in the nursery at Brixton Women's prison, ca. 1860.

Mayhew and Binny, *Criminal Prisons of London* (1862)

Reform and Retribution: An Illustrated History of American Prisons

John Howard

American Correctional Association

John Howard: the father of modern prison reform.

John Howard (1726-1790) was the leading light of eighteenth century prison reform. Devoted to humanitarian causes, Howard was en route to Portugal in 1755 to help earthquake victims when his ship was captured by the French, with whom England was then at war. Howard thus was introduced to prison conditions as an inmate in a French prison. Later, as a county sheriff and prison commissioner in his native England, he was appalled by the jail and prison conditions he found.

In the 1770s, Howard inspected prisons throughout England and Europe. His most important publication, *State of Prisons* (1777), surveyed European prison conditions, proposed reforms, and coined the word "penitentiary." He promoted numerous prison reforms including improving sanitation, classifying inmates, hiring qualified staff, eliminating corruption in prison management and discontinuing the practice of collecting fees from inmates. He successfully lobbied Parliament to enact many of his proposals.

Howard, who was equally interested in hospital reform, died in Russia in 1790 while working to improve Russian military hospitals. After his death, the John Howard Association kept his work alive and became one of England's premier prison reform societies. In the United States, an organization bearing his name was created in 1900 to help newly freed prisoners make the transition back into the community. The John Howard Association continues to be a respected advocate of prison reform.

Mayhew and Binny, *Criminal Prisons of London* (1862)

At Coldbath Fields Prison in Britain, inmates exercise in the prison yard (foreground), above them fellow inmates labor on treadmills.

2 Colonial and Revolutionary America

The thirteen British colonies in North America inherited British legal forms, including methods of punishment. They were also receptive to prison reforms being proposed in Europe during the eighteenth century. When the American Revolution ushered in independence for the United States in 1776, and the former colonies were free to establish new governments and criminal justice systems, the path was clear to develop prisons as the primary method for punishing offenders.

Federal Bureau of Prisons, *Handbook of Correctional Institution Design and Construction* (1949)

Public humiliation by such means as placing offenders in pillories was a favored sanction in Colonial America.

Sanctions in the Colonies

Like European countries, Colonial America in the 1600s and 1700s maintained facilities to confine offenders awaiting sentencing, but confinement itself, generally, was not the sentence. Corporal and capital punishment were the usual sentences for serious crimes.

Executions were carried out by such means as hanging, firing squads, burning at the stake, and—in one case of a supposed witch in Salem, Massachusetts—crushing. Capital crimes in many colonies included murder, manslaughter, rape, and kidnaping, but the small, tightly knit, and isolated settlements in the American wilderness also prescribed the death penalty for many morals offenses. In 1641, for example, the Massachusetts criminal code identified idolatry, witchcraft, blasphemy, and adultery as capital offenses. Branding and whipping were among the corporal punishments carried out in the colonies.

For lesser crimes, there was public humiliation. Throughout the colonies, towns maintained stocks and pillories in public gathering places. Locked in these devices, offenders were exposed to stares and ridicule.

The few jails that did exist—again, largely to detain those awaiting corporal or capital punishment—were unsanitary and understaffed. They indiscriminately held men and women of all ages, and those convicted of all sorts of crimes, together in large rooms. Mothers sometimes were accompanied into those wretched common rooms by their children.

Ruins of Simsbury Prison, Connecticut.

Federal Bureau of Prisons, *Handbook of Correctional Institution Design and Construction* (1949)

Reform and Retribution: An Illustrated History of American Prisons

Penn's Code

William Penn sailed from England to North America in 1682 to organize the colony of Pennsylvania. He had obtained a grant for the colony from King Charles II as repayment for generous financial loans the king had received from Penn's father.

Penn converted to the Quaker religion as a young man and quickly became an influential preacher. Persecuted for his religious convictions, he was imprisoned on several occasions. While incarcerated, he became a fervent critic of the brutal conditions he saw and experienced, and he began to develop ideas on how to reform the criminal justice process. As the first governor of Pennsylvania, he had an opportunity to put his ideas into practice.

The "Great Code," which he promulgated, permitted capital punishment for murder only—as compared with the more than 200 capital offenses in England. Penn's code clearly established incarceration as the fundamental form of punishment. It was a significant step forward. Houses of correction were mandated for each county in Pennsylvania, which would not charge inmates for food and accommodations but, instead, would be financed by the government and would require inmates to perform useful work. Other reforms included introduction of bail and the abolition of stocks and pillories.

Pennsylvania's legal reforms were too visionary for England's liking, and, after Penn's death in 1718, Queen Anne forced their repeal. In their place, Pennsylvania enacted the "Sanguinary Laws," so called for the bloodiness of their punishments. The death penalty was reinstated for numerous offenses, and the Sanguinary Laws also provided for corporal punishment.

The people of Pennsylvania had approved of Penn's "Great Code." As soon as they had the chance—when America declared its independence—they began restoring much of it.

Historical Society of Pennsylvania

William Penn, the founder of Pennsylvania, championed more humane methods of punishing offenders.

Benjamin Rush and the Philadelphia Prison Society

In 1787, shortly after the United States won its independence, the world's first prison reform organization was born in Philadelphia. The Philadelphia Society for the Alleviation of the Miseries of Public Prisons (or Philadelphia Prison Society) sought to alleviate the deplorable conditions in places of confinement by visiting the public prisons and jails on a regular basis, inquiring into inmates' circumstances, and reporting abuses. The organization continues to function, more than two centuries later, as the Pennsylvania Prison Society.

In some respects, it was heir to an earlier organization, the Philadelphia Society for Assisting Distressed Prisoners, which was in existence briefly during the 1770s. Whereas the earlier group concentrated on distributing food and clothing to inmates, the new Philadelphia Prison Society had a far-reaching agenda: to completely redesign Pennsylvania's prison system.

The driving force behind the society was Benjamin Rush, a prominent physician, social reformer, and statesman who represented Pennsylvania in the Continental Congress and was a signer of the Declaration of Independence. Members of the Society included other eminent Philadelphians, including Benjamin Franklin.

Federal Bureau of Prisons, *Handbook of Correctional Institution Design and Construction* (1949)

Dr. Benjamin Rush led the prison reform efforts in Pennsylvania during the late eighteenth century.

The Walnut Street Jail in Philadelphia. A wing of the prison erected in the 1790s contained America's first penitentiary.

Pennsylvania Prison Society

Rush believed that prisons should remove not only dangerous persons from society, and thereby prevent crime, but also that they should endeavor to reform inmates into law-abiding citizens.

Conditions at Philadelphia's Walnut Street Jail spurred Rush and the Society to action. Despite the repeal of the Sanguinary Laws and the establishment of incarceration as the principal form of punishment, Pennsylvania's prisons did not operate satisfactorily. One of the most troubling problems was the employment of inmates on work projects outside the prison walls. Chained together and wearing brightly colored uniforms, the prisoners were placed in a humiliating position. The Philadelphia Prison Society objected to that practice because it was degrading to the inmates, and also, it believed, to society itself. Further, because prison rations were so meager, prisoners used their public exposure to beg for food. Within the prisons, meanwhile, there was a dangerous lack of sanitation, inadequate supervision of inmates, and no real classification of inmates.

Rush and the Philadelphia Prison Society campaigned against these conditions, and in 1789 and 1790, the Pennsylvania State Legislature passed laws implementing reforms they had proposed. Those laws established the first modern penitentiary.

Floor plan of the Walnut Street Jail, featuring both congregate rooms and individual cells.

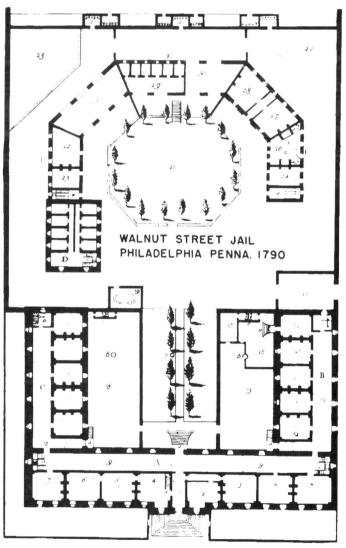

WALNUT STREET JAIL
PHILADELPHIA PENNA. 1790

Federal Bureau of Prisons, *Handbook of Correctional Institution Design and Construction* (1949)

America's First Prisons

There were numerous jails and proto-prisons in Colonial America, modeled largely on the workhouses and jails of England. Pennsylvania's Great Code, of course, provided for imprisonment as the punishment for most offenses. Other colonies erected detention facilities to hold individuals awaiting trial or sentencing. Massachusetts, for example, built a jail in Boston in 1635, and the Maryland Assembly authorized a small jail in 1662.

In 1775, Connecticut established a prison in an abandoned copper mine in Simsbury, which became the state prison following the Revolution. Sentences were tough—ten years on a first offense for burglary, for example—and conditions were abominable. Inmates were kept chained in underground cages that were badly crowded; thirty-two men could be crammed into a cage only twenty-one feet long, ten feet wide, and less than seven feet high. A riot occurred at the prison only a year after it opened.

Maine operated a similar prison, located in a quarry. Inmates in chains spent daylight hours cutting stone, and at night were forced into dark, unheated, underground chambers.

The first true prison in America, however, was Philadelphia's Walnut Street Jail. It was arguably the world's first penitentiary, because it carried out incarceration as punishment, implemented a rudimentary classification system, featured individual cells, and was intended to provide a place for offenders to do penance—hence the term "penitentiary."

Built in 1773 as the city jail for Philadelphia, the Walnut Street Jail initially held debtors, misdemeanants, and individuals awaiting trial or sentencing for more serious offenses. For a brief period during the American Revolution, the Continental Congress used the facility to house petty offenders and those who supported the British.

Pennsylvania Prison Society

This stamp was issued to finance construction of Philadelphia's Walnut Street Jail in the 1770s.

Under the statutes of 1789 and 1790, which the Philadelphia Prison Society had urged, the Pennsylvania state legislature established the facility as Pennsylvania's state prison, on an interim basis. The laws also provided for the addition of a new, three-story wing to the prison. It was that wing that became the prototype of the modern penitentiary. Convicted felons were housed in that wing—some in individual cells—separated from the rest of the inmate population. A work program was developed within the prison, with inmates engaged in handicrafts such as shoemaking, weaving, cutting and polishing marble, and grinding plaster of paris. Finally, through the work programs and the remorse and penitential reflection that was supposed to occur during incarceration, it was hoped that the inmates would undergo a period of correction; therefore, the Walnut Street Jail indeed had come to fit the definition of a "correctional" institution.

The Walnut Street Jail embodied many of the advances in prison administration that the Philadelphia Prison Society had championed and that John Howard had proposed years before. Public officials from around the United States flocked to see it and returned to their own jurisdictions to emulate it.

Newgate Prison, which opened in 1797 in New York City, in many respects was modeled on the Walnut Street Jail. There were single cells for the most dangerous inmates, and inmate work programs carried out within the prison's walls covered most of the institution's costs. Corporal punishment was forbidden. Wholesome meals were served, with daily menu changes, and Newgate established the first prison hospital and hired the first full-time prison physician. There were even the first flickers of genuine professionalism in the clearly defined qualifications and job assignments for staff members at Newgate.

Front elevation and floor plan of Newgate Prison.

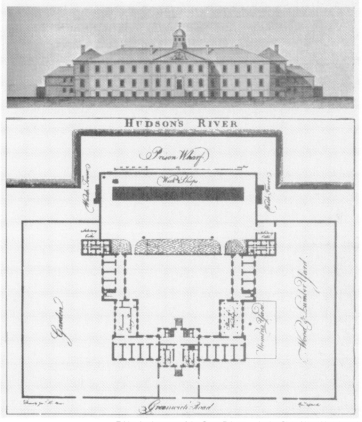

Eddy, *An Account of the State Prison . . . in the City of New York* (1801)

The underlying philosophy at Newgate was that criminals were redeemable. The institution's visionary warden, Thomas Eddy, established a school for convicts and held strict religious services with an eye toward rehabilitation.

It replicated the Walnut Street Jail in another area, however, that Warden Eddy regretted: it maintained single cells for only the most dangerous felons. The remainder of the population was kept in larger rooms that held as many as eight inmates. That led to significant disciplinary problems, culminating in 1802 with a terrible riot.

Thomas Eddy (1758-1827), warden of Newgate Prison.

Knapp, *The Life of Thomas Eddy* (1834)

Newgate Prison, New York City, 1797.

Federal Bureau of Prisons, *Handbook of Correctional Institution Design and Construction* (1949)

Other prisons of the period that were more or less inspired by the Walnut Street Jail and Newgate Prison included state prisons in Trenton, New Jersey (1798), Richmond, Virginia (1800), Charlestown, Massachusetts (1805), and Baltimore, Maryland (1811).

The Walnut Street Jail and Newgate Prison paved the way for the development of the modern prison. The era of the penitentiary was at hand.

Original buildings of the state prison in Trenton, New Jersey, erected in 1798.

Federal Bureau of Prisons, *Handbook of Correctional Institution Design and Construction* (1949)

Massachusetts Department of Corrections

The Massachusetts State Prison at Charlestown, erected in 1805, was inspired by the Walnut Street model.

THE QUAKER INFLUENCE

In both England and the United States, adherents of the Quaker religion were among the most dedicated and influential prison reformers of the eighteenth and nineteenth centuries. They believed that reformation or salvation should be the objective of punishment. They worked tirelessly for more humane prisons and rejected corporal and capital punishment.

The American penitentiary emerged largely due to the efforts of the Quakers. William Penn, who established Quakerism in North America, was Governor of colonial Pennsylvania when it made early attempts to establish incarceration as a humane and constructive alternative to other forms of punishment. In 1787, Quakers were among the founders of the Philadelphia Society for Alleviating the Miseries of Public Prisons, which was instrumental in bringing about the realization of the penitentiary concept at the Walnut Street Jail and Eastern State Penitentiary. New York businessman and philanthropist Thomas Eddy, warden of New York City's Newgate Prison, was a Quaker. His impact on prisons was so great that he has been called "America's John Howard." He and other New York Quakers formed the Society for the Prevention of Pauperism in the early 1800s, which endeavored to improve treatment of juvenile offenders and promote the development of single-cell prisons.

Quakers in England in the nineteenth century were no less active in working for better prisons, through such organizations as the Society for Diffusing Information on the Death Penalty and the Society for the Improvement of Prison Discipline. Elizabeth Gurney Fry (1780-1845) was the most notable of the English Quaker prison reformers. In the early decades of the nineteenth century, she crusaded for better prison conditions for women and established guidelines for the management and administration of women's prisons. She emphasized the need to furnish training and work skills in prison and personally provided religious counsel to female inmates.

Ironically, by the late twentieth century, many Quakers regretted Quakerism's historic involvement with prisons and contributions to the development of penitentiaries. A leading group of Quaker activists, the American Friends Service Committee, lamented in 1971 that "the horror that is the American prison system grew out of an eighteenth-century reform by Pennsylvania Quakers and others against the cruelty and futility of capital and corporal punishment." The committee concluded that "this two-hundred-year-old experiment has failed."

American Correctional Association

Elizabeth Gurney Fry. Her prison reforms of the early nineteenth century, and her humanitarian spirit, continued to be influential more than a century later.

3

The Rise of the Penitentiary

The modern definition of a penitentiary is a maximum-security penal institution: a prison with the highest walls, the strongest locks, the tightest restrictions, and the toughest inmates. Originally, however, the word "penitentiary" derives from "penance." A penitentiary was a place where offenders were sent to do penance for their crimes and attain redemption, through isolation, reflection, and hard work.

The Walnut Street Jail and Newgate Prison were America's first penitentiaries, but they really were only prototypes. As design flaws and program limitations became apparent, states moved during the 1800s to build massive penitentiaries that would correct those flaws.

Quickly, two rival categories of penitentiaries emerged: the Pennsylvania System and the Auburn System. Penitentiaries built and administered on one or the other system dominated penology in the United States for much of the nineteenth century.

Inmates are dwarfed by the medieval turrets at Joliet Penitentiary in Illinois.

Illinois Department of Corrections

The Pennsylvania System (Separate System)

The Walnut Street Jail was intended to serve as the Pennsylvania state prison only temporarily. It was replaced in 1829 when Pennsylvania opened the Eastern State Penitentiary. Also known as Cherry Hill, for the area of Philadelphia where it was located, Eastern State was designed by British-born architect John Haviland in harmony with principles endorsed by the Philadelphia Prison Society. Its philosophy and physical layout became a model for penitentiaries that conformed to what became known as the "Pennsylvania System." Because of its reliance on complete solitary confinement, the Pennsylvania System also was known as the "Separate System."

Operations at Eastern State were based on the conviction that solitary confinement was the most conducive method for helping offenders reform their behavior. Locked in their cells at all times, even taking their meals alone, inmates had contact only with staff members, representatives of the Philadelphia Prison Society, and chaplains. With so much solitude, prisoners presumably would spend their sentences meditating about their misdeeds, studying the Bible, and preparing to lead law-abiding lives after release.

Federal Bureau of Prisons, *Handbook of Correctional Institution Design and Construction* (1949)

John Haviland, architect of Eastern State and other American prisons of the early nineteenth century.

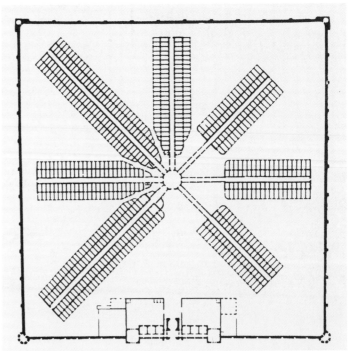

Floor plan showing radial cellblock design of Eastern State Penitentiary.

Federal Bureau of Prisons, *Handbook of Correctional Institution Design and Construction* (1949)

Moreover, solitary confinement would eliminate the interaction between convicted felons that prison administrators feared would reinforce patterns of criminal behavior. To ensure that inmates at Eastern State Penitentiary would not consort with each other, they were required to wear hoods or masks on those rare occasions when they were permitted outside their cells. Finally, proponents of the system theorized that solitary confinement would help prevent misconduct and facilitate inmate control.

The cellblocks at Eastern State radiated out from a central rotunda. A corridor ran down the center of each cellblock, with cells on either side of the corridor. Ground-level cells opened out onto small exercise yards, each of which was surrounded by a high stone fence. Because cells had exterior walls facing the outdoors, they were called "outside cells."

Even in 1829, the cells at Eastern State had plumbing. The cells were also quite large, partly to enable inmates to work at various handicrafts. Prisoners made shoes, wove and dyed cloth products, caned chairs, and rolled cigars. Those products were sold to defray prison costs.

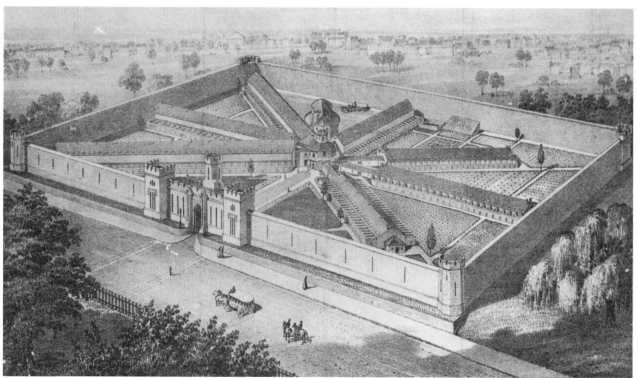

American Correctional Association

Long cellhouses radiating out from a central rotunda were a distinctive feature of Eastern State Penitentiary's layout. Enclosed yards outside each cell enabled inmates to exercise in fresh air while maintaining the rigid "separate system."

The Dickens Fellowship (London)

Renowned British novelist Charles Dickens wrote critically about Eastern State after visiting the United States in the 1840s.

The Pennsylvania System was beset with serious problems. Its philosophical basis, solitary confinement, was the subject of a bitter debate among prison experts. Instead of promoting reflection and rehabilitation, there was evidence that solitary confinement caused psychological distress, and even insanity. When Charles Dickens visited Eastern State in 1842, he praised the facility for its cleanliness and orderliness, but deplored the "strict and hopeless confinement," which he characterized as "cruel and wrong." Dickens considered solitary confinement's "slow and daily tampering with the mysteries of the brain to be immeasurably worse than any torture of the body."

There were also significant economic drawbacks. First, it was tremendously expensive to maintain individual cells for each inmate. By the late nineteenth century, even Eastern State had to double-bunk inmates. Second, preindustrial handicraft production, with inmates working by themselves, simply could not produce the type of merchandise, or merchandise in sufficient quantities, to generate a large enough income to support prison operations.

Typical cell at Eastern State Penitentiary.

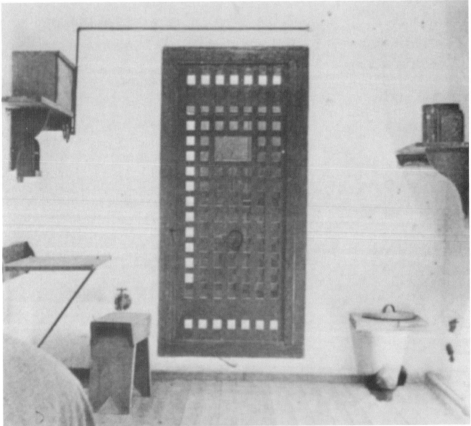

Vaux, *Brief Sketch of the Origin and History of the State Penitentiary* (1872)

Cassidy, *Warden Cassidy on Prisons and Convicts* (1897)

Interior of Eastern State's central rotunda, 1880s, with cellblocks branching out on the left and right.

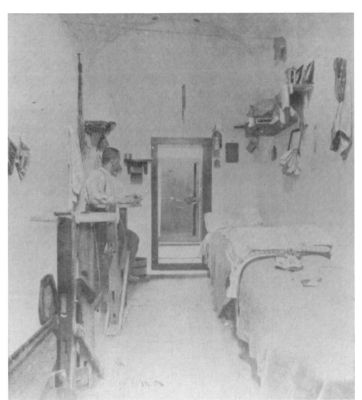

Cassidy, *Warden Cassidy on Prisons and Convicts* (1897)

Initially intended to hold inmates in solitary confinement, by the later nineteenth century Eastern State cells were occupied by two inmates.

The Pennsylvania System had its highest expression in Eastern State, and there were attempts to copy it. On the other side of Pennsylvania from Philadelphia, the Western State Penitentiary, in Pittsburgh, had been opened eight years before Eastern State's. It had been a failure, and was rebuilt in the 1830s with an outside cell design by Haviland. It also adopted Eastern State's programs. Cellhouses, in accordance with the Pennsylvania System, also were built in Trenton, New Jersey, and Baltimore, Maryland. Because of the various problems associated with it, however, the Pennsylvania System was not as influential as its rival, the Auburn System.

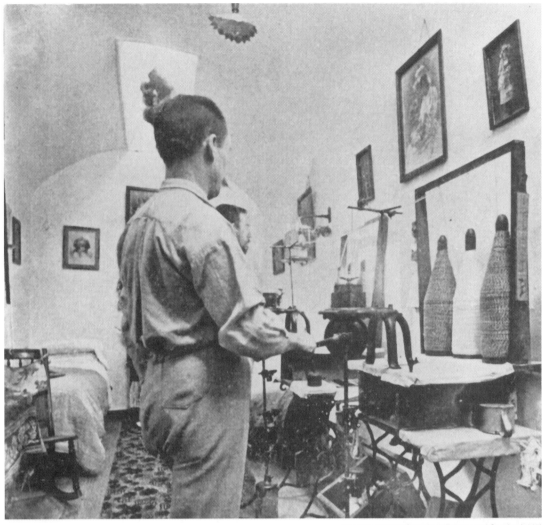

Cassidy, *Warden Cassidy on Prisons and Convicts* (1897)

Work assignments at Eastern State—such as knitting hosiery and caning chairs—took place in large cells rather than factories.

Roberts Vaux (1786-1836) was a prominent member of the Philadelphia Prison Society and one of the guiding forces behind the establishment of Eastern State Penitentiary.

Son Richard Vaux (far right) (1816-1895) carried on his father's work by serving as President of Eastern State Penitentiary's Board of Trustees.

American Correctional Association

American Correctional Association

American Correctional Association

Eastern State Penitentiary about the time of its opening, in 1829.

Cassidy, *Warden Cassidy on Prisons and Convicts* (1897)

Michael Cassidy, warden of Eastern State Penitentiary, 1881-1900

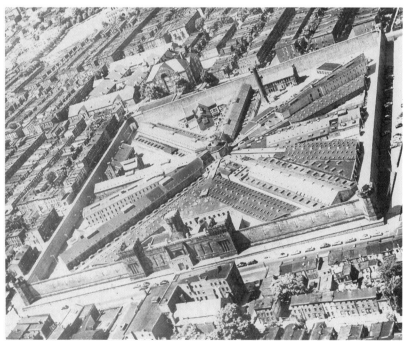

American Correctional Association

By 1958, Eastern State Penitentiary was hemmed in by teeming Philadelphia neighborhoods, as shown in this aerial photograph. The prison had abandoned its reliance on solitary confinement nearly a century earlier. Additional structures built to accommodate increasing numbers of inmates eliminated the yards and gardens that had existed between the cellhouses. The facility was cramped, over-crowded, and dilapidated. Twelve years later it would be closed, after almost 150 years of operation.

The Auburn System
(Congregate System)

In 1817, crowding at Newgate Prison prompted New York to open a new state prison in Auburn. Built between 1816 and 1825, and expanded thereafter, Auburn was the birthplace of the "Congregate System" of inmate management. The Congregate or Auburn System came to dominate American corrections.

Like the Pennsylvania System, the Auburn System housed inmates in individual cells and prohibited communications among inmates. Unlike the Pennsylvania System, the Auburn System restricted inmates to their cells only during evening hours. By day, inmates were fed together in large mess halls and worked together in large shops or factories.

The Auburn Prison in New York, which pioneered the "inside" cellblock design.

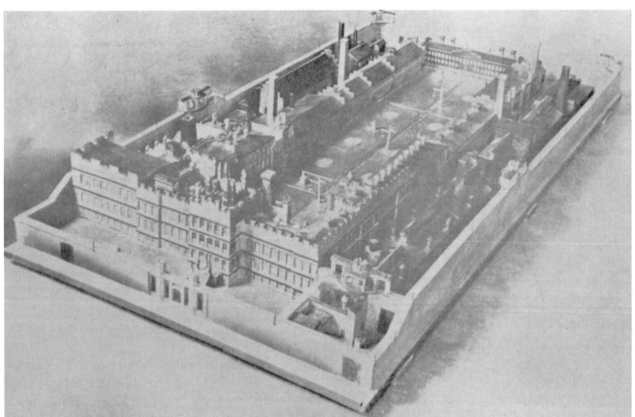

Federal Bureau of Prisons, *Handbook of Correctional Institution Design and Construction* (1949)

Probably the greatest advantage of the Auburn System was economic. Because inmates were in their cells only at night, the cells did not need to be as large as those under the Pennsylvania System. It was less expensive to build prisons with smaller cells because more inmates could be housed in a given area. Not only did Auburn-style prisons cost less, they also could bring in considerably more money. Permitting inmates to work in large groups, rather than individually, meant a transition from handicraft production to industrial production—which was more efficient and profitable.

Front entrance of the Auburn Prison (photograph taken ca. 1940).

Federal Bureau of Prisons, *Handbook of Correctional Institution Design and Construction* (1949)

Congregate labor made inmates an economic asset, and private business interests quickly moved to take advantage. As early as 1825, private companies had begun the practice of availing themselves of the benefits of inmate labor. Under the "contract" system, which appeared largely in the North, companies paid fees to states in exchange for the labor of inmates who worked in prison factories. Under the "lease" system, which became prevalent in the South and West, states actually leased prisoners out to private firms. Instead of working in prison factories, the inmates worked at privately owned factories, mines, logging camps, and plantations.

Auburn's main yard, shown here in the 1880s, gave inmates some relief from the grim cellhouses and harsh regimentation.

New York Department of Corrections

Reform and Retribution: An Illustrated History of American Prisons

Discipline was an area where the Auburn System compared unfavorably with the Pennsylvania System. With hundreds of inmates congregated together for much of the day, officials at Auburn-style penitentiaries felt compelled to introduce harsh measures to maintain control. Inmates ate and worked together in total silence. The need to maintain control under the Auburn System also gave rise to striped uniforms and the lockstep.

Prisoners march in lockstep across the yard at Joliet Penitentiary, Illinois, ca. 1900.

Illinois Department of Corrections

Auburn-style interior cellblock, 1852.

Finley, *Memorials of Prison Life* (1854)

To help maintain discipline under the "congregate system," Auburn inmates in the 1820s wore easily recognized striped uniforms, and marched in lockstep.

Barber, *Historical Collections of the State of New York* (1840)

Reform and Retribution: An Illustrated History of American Prisons

Illustrated London News (February 16, 1876)

Striped uniforms and the lockstep continued
as basic features in Auburn-style prisons in
the mid and late nineteenth century.

Dudding, *The Trail of the Dead Years* (1932)

Severe physical punishment could be meted out for infractions. Ironically, whereas the penitentiary concept was developed as a humane alternative to corporal punishment, corporal punishment returned as a device to manage inmates in penitentiaries based on the Auburn System.

At an unidentified prison about 1900, inmates with shaven heads and striped uniforms await flogging for disciplinary infractions.

Dudding, *The Trail of the Dead Years* (1932)

Example of Auburn-style "inside" cellblock ca. 1925. Inmates at Great Meadow Prison, Comstock, New York, await the opening of cell doors by an officer at a locking device that controlled all the grilles on the tier.

(Facing page) The Joliet Penitentiary in Illinois featured a combination whipping post and pillory around 1900.

New York Department of Corrections

Reform and Retribution: An Illustrated History of American Prisons

Illinois Department of Corrections

Architecturally, the Auburn System was dramatically different from the Pennsylvania System. Cellblocks consisted of long, multi-tiered, double rows of cells that were placed back to back. The cells did not have exterior walls; instead, they were completely surrounded by a corridor or range. Cellblocks literally were enclosed within a larger building. For that reason, Auburn-style cells are called "inside cells," in contrast with the outside cells in Pennsylvania-style prisons. Cellhouse architecture based on the Auburn model became the standard for a century. Inside cellblocks are still in use throughout the United States, and they are undoubtedly the type of prison architecture most familiar to the general public.

Penitentiaries erected in the nineteenth century tended to be imposing Gothic, castle-like monuments, such as the Maryland State Penitentiary in Baltimore.

Maryland Department of Corrections

Back-to-back cells run down the middle of cellblocks with corridors or ranges on either side of Auburn cellblocks.

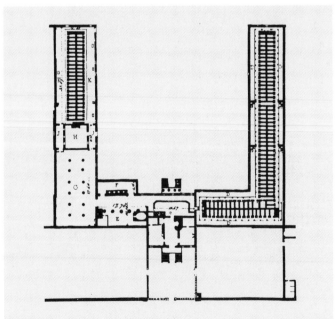

Federal Bureau of Prisons, *Handbook of Correctional Institution Design and Construction* (1949)

Reform and Retribution: An Illustrated History of American Prisons

Another aspect of Auburn-style prison architecture was that it tended to be on a grand scale. The fortress-like walls, the imposing towers, and the monumental, Gothic structures enhanced security and made a vivid statement about the power and authority of the state. Critics in the twentieth century also claimed that such massive prison architecture was demoralizing and dehumanizing for occupants.

Between the 1820s and the 1870s, nearly thirty state prisons were erected and operated following the Auburn model. Others—such as the New Jersey State Prison at Trenton—converted from the Pennsylvania System to the Auburn System. Northeastern and midwestern states lagged behind, although Texas, Mississippi, Louisiana, and Arkansas built Auburn-style prisons before the Civil War. Even Pennsylvania, itself, moved away from the Pennsylvania System in the 1870s with the erection of a new Western State Penitentiary in Pittsburgh built along Auburn lines.

Gothic facade of Indiana's Jefferson Prison, erected in the nineteenth century.

Indiana Department of Corrections

Barber, *Historical Collections of the State of New York* (1840)

Sing Sing Prison in Ossining, New York, was
built in the 1840s on the Auburn model.

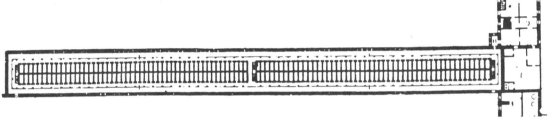

The Auburn-style cellblocks at Sing Sing
were among the longest ever built.

Federal Bureau of Prisons, *Handbook of Correctional Institution Design and Construction* (1949)

Federal Bureau of Prisons, *Handbook of Correctional Institution Design and Construction* (1949)

By 1927, when this photograph was taken at Auburn, crowding had made it necessary to place additional bunks on the bottom range, across from the cells.

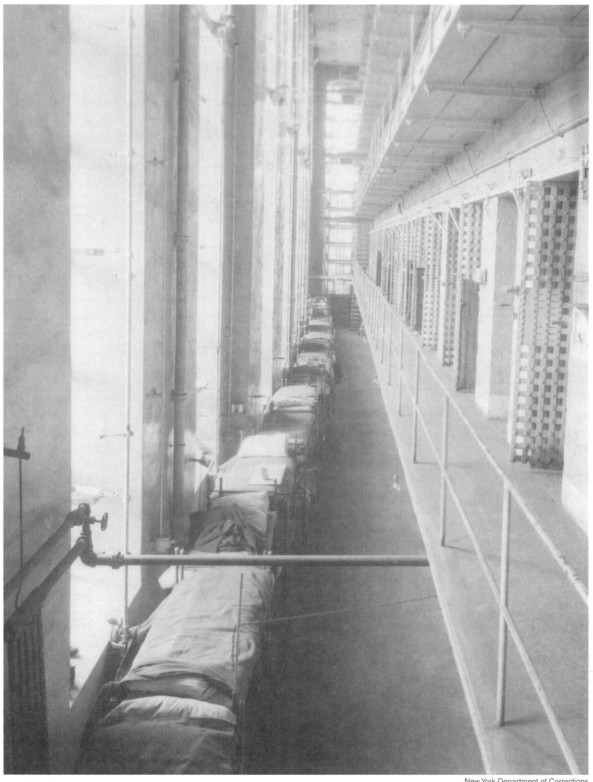

New York Department of Corrections

The Civil War and its Aftermath

The Civil War had several direct and indirect influences on the history of American corrections. The most dramatic and shocking was the appearance of prisons that were probably the most inhumane of any on United States' soil: prisoner of war camps operated by both the Union and the Confederacy.

Although prisoner exchanges were not unusual during the war, large numbers of combatants were incarcerated for lengthy periods. Some prisoners of war, as well as deserters, were housed in state penitentiaries. The majority, however, were held in camps under miserable conditions. Prisoners of war often were completely exposed to the elements, or sheltered only by small, flimsy tents. Food was scarce and what there was tended to be monotonous. Many prisoners of war literally starved to death, and many of those who survived incarceration were left horribly sick and emaciated from malnourishment. Sanitation and medical care were inadequate or nonexistent, and disease was rampant.

The horrendous prison camp conditions prevailed both in the North and the South. A Confederate prisoner compared Camp Douglas in Chicago to a "cattle yard" and shuddered at Confederate corpses "piled one upon the other, as . . . frozen mutton carcasses are carted from the docks!"

The most notorious camp, however, was operated by the Confederacy in Andersonville, Georgia. As many as 32,000 Union soldiers were crammed into an open-air prison so small that there was only six feet of space per man. In a period of just six months in 1864, 8,589 Yankees died at Andersonville. Andersonville's commandant was the only person tried and executed after the Civil War for war crimes.

The Civil War had an impact on prisons that went beyond the horrors of Andersonville and Camp Douglas. There was a sudden escalation in the prison population as soon as the war ended, partly because of the demobilization of millions of Union and Confederate servicemen.

Isaac W. K. Handy, *United States Bonds* (1874)

Bread crusts being thrown to Confederate prisoners at the Union's Fort Delaware prison camp in Maryland, August 1863.

Reform and Retribution: An Illustrated History of American Prisons

Library of Congress (photo by A. J. Riddle, 1865)

Simple tents and other crude shelters at Andersonville Prison Camp in Georgia (1865) lie beyond the long, wooden latrine that contaminated the water supply for the thousands of Union prisoners of war confined there.

The South was particularly hard hit. Prison development in the southern states had been derailed by the Civil War. When the war ended, the small and dilapidated facilities were ill-equipped to handle the influx of new inmates. Moreover, the emancipation of slaves meant that an entirely new group became part of the civilian population and subject to imprisonment for criminal violations. Previously, slaves generally were punished on the plantations where they lived and did not pass into the criminal justice systems of the South.

Overcrowding brought the flaws of Auburn-style prisons—the harsh discipline, the abuse of convict labor—into full relief. Again, the problems were especially pronounced in the South. Unable to handle the growing inmate population in their own prisons, and lacking sufficient resources to build new ones, southern states drastically increased their reliance on convict leasing.

Convict leasing in the post-Civil War South meant cramped jail wagons, shotgun-toting and pistol-packing guards, dogs for chasing down would-be escapees, and back-breaking work cutting timber, building roads, and picking cotton.

Library of Congress

Louisiana Department of Corrections

Contractors who leased inmates from southern prisons housed them in squalid camps or cramped and filthy wagons, and forced them to perform long hours of back-breaking toil on cotton plantations, sugar plantations, quarries, roads, and canals, and elsewhere. In practice, convict leasing in the South became a very convenient and legally permissible substitute for slavery.

The conclusion of the Civil War also ushered in a period of breathtaking growth in the United States. The West was settled, the transcontinental railroad was laid, immigrants flooded into the country, industrial activity burgeoned, and the financial community expanded. Much of the growth was spearheaded by the federal government, which subsidized railroad construction, enacted homestead laws to help the settlers, and encouraged industrial expansion. As the country and its population grew, so too did the number of federal laws and responsibilities. With that growth came an increase in the number of individuals who broke federal laws; accordingly, the federal government faced the prospect of having to develop its own system of prisons.

Prison crowding, exacerbation of Auburn System flaws, the transformation of convict leasing into a new form of slavery, and the need for the federal government to play a role in corrections—all of those factors made the post-Civil War period ripe for upheaval in prison operations.

American Correctional Association

Panopticon Prisons

*A*round 1800, three architectural styles for prisons appeared. The Pennsylvania System featured outside cells on either side of long corridors radiating out from a central rotunda. The Auburn style featured multiple tiers of inside cells surrounded by a corridor or range. The third style was the Panopticon design.

The great English philosopher and scholar, Jeremy Bentham (1748-1831), originated the Panopticon design in 1791. It consisted of multiple stories of outside cells, built in a large circle, and facing onto an interior well or courtyard. In the center of the well, like the hub in the center of a wheel, was an enclosed guard's station.

Bentham theorized that the design could improve prison security and enhance inmates' propensity for moral reflection. With every cell visible from the central vantage point, constant supervision was possible. Inmates, knowing they could be seen at all times, supposedly would become more circumspect and eventually would internalize patterns of better behavior. The guard's station also served as a convenient location for giving sermons and other religious instruction to the entire cellblock at once.

Federal Bureau of Prisons, *Handbook of Correctional Institution Design and Construction* (1949)

Jeremy Bentham, originator of the Panopticon design. His plan of 1791 is shown at the right.

The Virginia Penitentiary in Richmond (built in 1800) was a modified, semicircular version of the Panopticon design.

Federal Bureau of Prisons, *Handbook of Correctional Institution Design and Construction* (1949)

American Correctional Association

Illinois' Stateville Penitentiary, 1936, with round cellhouses based on Bentham's plan.

Several European prisons and even a few in the United States were built on the Panopticon design. The semi-circular Virginia State Prison in Richmond, built in 1800, was a modified version of the Panopticon design. The Western State Penitentiary in Pittsburgh, Pennsylvania, was built in 1826 as a Panopticon prison, but it was such a crashing failure that after only a few years it was demolished and an Auburn-style prison erected in its place. The grandest example of the Panopticon design in the United States was the elephantine Stateville Penitentiary in Illinois, which was built in 1919.

Layout of original Western State Penitentiary in Pittsburgh.

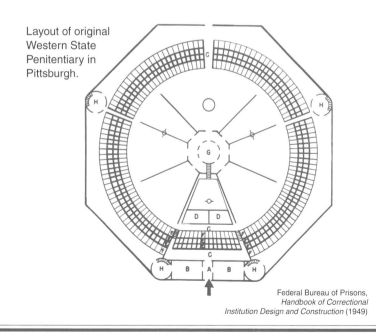

Federal Bureau of Prisons, *Handbook of Correctional Institution Design and Construction* (1949)

Interior of Stateville's inmate dining room, ca. 1953, with three-story guard tower at the hub.

Illinois Department of Corrections

Cellblock at Stateville Penitentiary.

Federal Bureau of Prisons, *Handbook of Correctional Institution Design and Construction* (1949)

Reform and Retribution: An Illustrated History of American Prisons

4

The Reformatory Era

American Correctional Association

Training course in drafting at Elmira Reformatory (1909).

The penitentiary concept included two fundamental elements: first, imprisonment should be society's primary form of punishment; and second, imprisonment should help inmates to become reformed. From the late 1700s through the mid-1800s, the penitentiary had succeeded well at the punishment aspect of its mission, but it had done little to help reform inmates.

Revulsion with the harsher and more punitive features of penitentiaries based on the Auburn model, outrage over the abuses of convict leasing, and a desire to transform prisons into healthier, more constructive, and more rehabilitation-oriented institutions created a mood for change in the field of corrections during the latter decades of the nineteenth century. It spawned the National Prison Association—forerunner of the American Correctional Association—and it gave rise to a new kind of prison: the reformatory.

New Ideas from the Old World

In the eighteenth century, Benjamin Rush and other prison reformers in the United States drew on the ideas of European thinkers such as John Howard, Cesare Beccaria, and Jeremy Bentham. Similarly, ideas and developments in Europe during the nineteenth century proved highly influential in the United States.

In France, Charles Lucas published several books in the 1830s calling for programs of curative treatment in prison, rather than just pure discipline, that offered incentives for inmates to reform. The notion of stimulating rehabilitation through incentives was championed further by Dublin's Archbishop Richard Whatley (1787-1863), Bonneville de Marsangy of France, and English prison reformers such as Mary Carpenter (1807-1877), and the Hill brothers, Frederick (1803-1896) and Matthew (1790-1872).

A critical element of the curative regime that those reformers proposed was that prisoners should be released only upon achieving rehabilitation, as demonstrated by good behavior while incarcerated. Behavioral transformation was viewed as more important than having an inmate serve a fixed sentence. Those who demonstrated good behavior should be released early; those who did not should remain in prison longer. According to Frederick Hill, prison should be a "moral hospital" where prisoners would be incarcerated until they were "cured of their bad habits."

Elmira Reformatory, in New York, became the prototype for the adult reformatory after it opened in 1876.

Federal Bureau of Prisons, *Handbook of Correctional Institution Design and Construction* (1949)

New York Department of Corrections

Training courses at the Elmira Reformatory included sign painting and ceiling frieze decorating (1898).

The idea of inmates remaining incarcerated until they were "cured"—which could be a shorter period than a fixed sentence but could also be a longer period—gave rise to such concepts as commutation of sentences for good behavior, parole, and indeterminate sentencing. In the 1830s, there were two successful but short-lived practical examples of the philosophy of offering early release as an incentive for good behavior (and theoretically rehabilitation): Spain's Valencia Prison, under the administration of Colonel Manuel Montesinos, and Australia's Norfolk Island prison colony, under Captain Alexander Maconochie (1777-1861). The practice finally took root, however, in Ireland.

The Irish prison system developed in the middle of the nineteenth century by Sir Joshua Jebb (1793-1863) and Sir Walter Crofton (1815-1897) was considered the most enlightened of its day. It combined religious, educational, and work programs with a graduated classification system, through which an inmate had to progress before being released. Inmates began their sentences in solitary confinement, with reduced rations and no work assignments. Good conduct won advancement to the next stage of incarceration, which included congregate labor and improved rations. In the final stage, the inmate was moved into a less restrictive prison environment, had a job assignment in the community, and could earn credits toward early release—again, if conduct seemed to indicate that the inmate had achieved rehabilitation.

Although the Irish system won international acclaim, the new ideas caught on slowly in Europe. They found a more receptive audience in the United States.

Library of Congress (photo by Smith and Miller)

The impressive uniforms and proud expressions of officers at the Charlestown State Prison in Massachusetts (1896) are reflective of the strong sense of professionalism that had appeared in corrections by the late nineteenth century, and which was one of the reasons for the establishment of the National Prison Association in 1870.

American Correctional Association

Enoch Cobb Wines was Secretary of the New York Prison Association for seventeen years and one of the founders of the National Prison Association.

New York Department of Corrections

William M. F. Round, first Secretary of the National Prison Association.

National Prison Association

In 1867, the New York Prison Association commissioned Enoch Cobb Wines (1806-1879) and Theodore Dwight (1822-1892) to study prison conditions throughout the United States and Canada. In their report, Wines and Dwight condemned many of the practices they found and called for "judicious revision."

They called for physical improvements in prisons, such as larger cells and better sanitation. They also advocated better training for officers and regular inspections by state boards. They attacked the corporal punishments that were so commonly used to deal with prison misconduct, and which could include whipping, placing an inmate in an iron yoke, chaining prisoners down in a box and drenching them with powerful bursts of water (the "water cure"), and other painful indignities. Finally, Wines and Dwight advocated curative measures and incentives to rehabilitate inmates, including religious and educational offerings, and opportunities to earn early release.

Wines and Dwight were at the center of a prison reform movement that was emerging in the United States, and they were greatly inspired by the Irish system. Having seen conditions in American prisons, and having learned about the ideas emanating from Europe, Wines, Dwight, Benjamin Franklin Sanborn (1831-1917), Samuel Gridley Howe (1802-1876), and others were ready to undertake an aggressive campaign to transform American corrections.

Among the first fruit borne by that campaign was the greater centralization of authority over prisons in state boards of charity. By 1869, state boards in Massachusetts, Ohio, Pennsylvania, Rhode Island, and Illinois had assumed responsibility from local authorities and were beginning the process of making improvements and regular inspections.

The reform movement was crystallized in 1870 with the formation of the National Prison Association. Meeting in Cincinnati, the first Congress of the National Prison Association was attended by 130 delegates from 24 states, Canada, South America, and Europe. Sir Walter Crofton spoke to the Congress about his Irish system, and others made presentations on such topics as prison hygiene, sanitation, and classification.

The Congress was highlighted by the adoption of a Declaration of Principles, which strongly endorsed the reformatory concept, indeterminate sentencing, separate facilities for women and for juveniles, classification, centralized prison management in each state, and the Irish system. The Declaration called for abolition of convict leasing, improvement of prison architecture, establishment of prison schools and hospitals, job training for staff, and rewards for good conduct by inmates. It stated that "Reformation, not vindictive suffering" was the goal of incarceration, and proposed social training, industrial training, education, and religious instruction as the means to accomplish reformation.

American Correctional Association

Rutherford B. Hayes, President of the National Prison Association from 1883-1893, became a champion of prison reform following his administration as President of the United States.

Although Wines was possibly the greatest force behind the National Prison Association, the organization's most prominent member was Rutherford B. Hayes (1822-1893). Nationally renowned as a Civil War general, Governor of Ohio, and, from 1877 to 1881, President of the United States, Hayes concluded his distinguished career of public service as President of the National Prison Association from 1883 until his death ten years later.

Despite the enthusiasm and high ideals of its founders, the power of the National Prison Association quickly waned as it ran up against resistance, met with early failures, and dissipated its influence in the United States by becoming too entangled in the international prison reform movement. Nonetheless, the organization survived and evolved into the American Prison Association and then the American Correctional Association. Through its yearly Congresses, and the voluminous literature it produced, it played an important role in promoting the development of the reformatory, which was the next great step in the evolution of American corrections following the appearance of the penitentiary.

The Reformatory

American Correctional Association

Zebulon Brockway, Elmira's founding warden, earned a reputation for humanitarianism and progressive innovations in corrections that endured for more than a century; his reputation behind Elmira's walls as "Paddler Brockway" was less well known.

Zebulon Brockway (1827-1920) was the most influential warden of his generation. Driven by a strong religious faith in the redeemability of criminals, he was the founder of the American Reformatory System—also known as the Elmira System, for the prison in Elmira, New York, where Brockway established the first reformatory. The Elmira System quickly took center stage in American corrections, displacing the Pennsylvania and Auburn Systems.

Brockway first tried to introduce rehabilitative techniques in the 1860s at the Detroit House of Corrections. He became one of the most vigorous proponents of reform and an early member of the National Prison Association. He spoke at the historic 1870 National Prison Congress, presenting a well-received paper on the "Ideal for a True Prison System for a State." During his address, Brockway proclaimed that the object of prison should not be punishment, but rather "the protection of society by the prevention of crime and the reformation of criminals."

In 1876, Brockway became superintendent of Elmira Reformatory. He moved quickly to create an institution that was consistent with the National Prison Association's Declaration of Principles.

Although it retained the Auburn-style architecture, including inside cells, Elmira Reformatory rejected many aspects of the Auburn System. In theory, at least—and to some extent in practice—Elmira did away with corporal punishment, striped uniforms, the lockstep, the silent system, and other blatant efforts to humiliate or degrade inmates.

Classroom in unidentified prison, 1900.

American Correctional Association

New York Department of Corrections

Elmira training course in blacksmithing
(1898).

At the same time, Elmira Reformatory introduced a series of
new programs and other innovations. An academic program, with
teachers and guest lecturers from local schools and a nearby college, included courses on general subjects, as well as religion,
ethics, and industrial arts. There was vocational training in tailor-
ing, plumbing, telegraphy, and printing. Other programs and activities included a band, an inmate newspaper, daily calisthenics,
and organized athletics.

A work program in which private businesses purchased inmate
labor was not terribly different from contract labor operations at
other prisons, except insofar as it was considered part of Elmira's
vocational training effort. After state law prohibited contract labor schemes, Elmira's workshops were turned into trade schools,
and military drill practice replaced work assignments.

Borrowing from Maconochie's prison colony in Australia and
Crofton's Irish prison system, Brockway classified inmates into
three grades. Discipline problems and inmates who resisted the
rehabilitation efforts were relegated to the lowest grade. Those
who responded well to the program could be advanced through an
intermediate grade to the highest grade, where they enjoyed such

privileges as receiving visitors and earning credits—or "marks"—for early release. Inmates were sent to Elmira with indeterminate sentences. Sentences set maximum limits on the amount of time an inmate could serve, but Elmira officials had authority to release inmates earlier than that, based on good conduct and evidence of rehabilitation.

Eventually, problems emerged at Elmira that compromised its stated goal of rehabilitating offenders. There was a lack of funding, in common with other prisons, and the Auburn-style architecture was ill-suited to a reformatory program. The three-grade classification system, meanwhile, came to be used less as a tool for rehabilitation and more as a disciplinary structure. Further, about one-third of the inmates were repeat offenders, despite Brockway's desire to concentrate exclusively on first-time offenders who would be more receptive to rehabilitative programs.

New York Department of Corrections

Inmates marching in a military drill at Elmira Reformatory, 1880s—a precursor of twentieth century prison boot camps (see Chapter 9).

Moreover, Brockway himself may not have lived up to his own ideals. Surprisingly, Brockway permitted corporal punishment which was so common and barbaric for even the slightest of infractions that he earned the nickname "Paddler Brockway." There was compelling evidence of mismanagement at Elmira, incompetent medical treatment, and the officially sanctioned terrorization of weaker inmates by stronger ones.

Ohio Department of Correction

Prisons inspired by the Elmira Reformatory model included the Ohio Reformatory in Mansfield (above) and the Massachusetts Reformatory in Concord (below).

American Correctional Association

Those very serious shortcomings, however, do not diminish the impact of Brockway and Elmira. Between 1876 and 1913, seventeen states built adult reformatories. Reformatories at Ionia, Michigan; Concord, Massachusetts; Huntington, Pennsylvania; St. Cloud, Minnesota; Mansfield, Ohio; and Rahway, New Jersey, were some of the most significant from the reformatory era. Although those institutions were built like Auburn-style penitentiaries, newer reformatories by the 1920s were giving rise to new types of prison architecture that emphasized campus-like facilities instead of massive, forbidding fortresses. Considerable progress also was made in the development of reformatories for women (see Chapter 5).

Reformatories raised standards in corrections, but in the late nineteenth century, they were the exception rather than the rule. The majority of prisons and jails were crude, overcrowded, and punishment-oriented. Disciplinary practices were cruel, staff often were less likely to be professional and competent than politically appointed, and inmate labor was callously exploited. Those unsatisfactory conditions were especially pronounced in the South, which devoted fewer resources than other regions to prisons, schools, roads, or public undertakings of any kind.

American Correctional Association

About 1899, the Auburn-style cell-house of the United States Penitentiary at Leavenworth arose from the Kansas plains.

Slowly, however, reformatories even came to influence other types of penal institutions. Increasingly, prisons that were not actually reformatories dispensed with the lockstep, the silent system, corporal punishment, and other rigorous, regimented features of the Auburn System, and adopted features pioneered at Elmira. Except for the heavy emphasis on security, even maximum-security penitentiaries by the middle of the twentieth century resembled Elmira more than Auburn.

The reality of Brockway and Elmira was not as lustrous as the long-accepted image of Brockway and Elmira. But, the ideas that Brockway espoused—and which he put into practice, more or less, at Elmira—had a powerful impact on American corrections. That impact was not limited to the many reformatories that sprang up to emulate Elmira, but extended to prisons of all types.

Federal Bureau of Prisons

Every morning, federal prisoners marched from the military prison at Fort Leavenworth to work behind a temporary stockade fence on the construction of their future home, the new United States Penitentiary (ca. 1897).

The Three Prisons Act and the Origins of Federal Corrections

During the first century of American independence, as the Pennsylvania, Auburn, and Elmira Systems were evolving, and when American prisons included some of the most advanced in the western world, the United States federal government played virtually no role in corrections.

Until the end of the nineteenth century, the federal government was so small, and there were so few federal criminals, that Congress and the Justice Department deemed it unnecessary to maintain any federal prisons. There simply were not enough federal offenders to justify the cost. Instead, in accordance with the Judiciary Act of 1789, the federal government paid fees to state prisons and county jails to incarcerate the comparative handful of individuals convicted of violating federal statutes.

The federal government did maintain army stockades and navy brigs to house court-martialed military personnel, U.S. Marshal's offices generally had a few jail cells for holding pretrial detainees, and the United States government briefly operated a penitentiary in Washington, D.C. during the mid-nineteenth century, mainly for local offenders in that city. Apart from that, there were no federal prisons.

As the nineteenth century was drawing to a close, however, the practice of incarcerating federal offenders in state and county institutions was becoming obsolete. Three factors led to the demise of that system.

Inmates build a cellhouse at the United States Penitentiary at Atlanta, ca. 1901.

Federal Bureau of Prisons

Federal Bureau of Prisons

Staff of the United States Penitentiary at McNeil Island, in its entirety, about 1900. Warden Gilbert Palmer, third from left.

First, the growing population and the increasing number of federal laws meant a rise in the number of federal offenders. State prisons that already were crowded did not have enough bedspace to keep taking in federal prisoners. Second, conditions in some of the state prisons were so wretched that many members of Congress and officials of the Justice Department became opposed to sending federal prisoners to them. Finally, the national outcry against convict labor-leasing arrangements that were prevalent in state prisons led to enactment of a federal law in 1887 that prohibited the leasing of federal prisoners. That law removed much of the economic incentive for state prisons and county jails to incarcerate federal prisoners, and they began to resist accepting them.

In 1891, Congress responded by passing the Three Prisons Act, authorizing establishment of three United States penitentiaries. The first was opened in 1895, and located in the old military prison at Fort Leavenworth, Kansas, which the Army had turned over to the Justice Department temporarily. Every morning, inmates were marched down Metropolitan Avenue to build the permanent Leavenworth Penitentiary, which was fully operational by 1906. The United States Penitentiary at Atlanta opened in 1902, and in 1907, a former territorial prison on McNeil Island in Puget Sound, Washington, which had been operating for several years as a U.S. Marshal's jail, was designated as the third United States penitentiary.

Federal Bureau of Prisons

The United States Penitentiary at McNeil Island, Washington, was originally a territorial prison. The gabled cellhouse on the left and its Auburn-style inside cells were identical to the designs of other nineteenth century territorial prisons, including the ones at Deer Lodge, Montana; Laramie, Wyoming; and Canon City, Colorado.

The new prisons were beset with an array of problems that were not solved until the formation of the Federal Bureau of Prisons in 1930. Wardens were political appointees; many staff members lacked training and experience; the institutions quickly became crowded; and there was a serious lack of funding. The only horses Leavenworth Penitentiary could afford to buy, for example, were so old and broken down that there was genuine speculation that escaping inmates could outrun them.

Nonetheless, the Three Prisons Act represented the inauguration of the federal prison system, and was an important milestone in the prison reform movement of the nineteenth century.

Officer sporting fashionable mutton-chop whiskers relaxes outside pad-locked door to cellhouse at the United States Penitentiary at McNeil Island, ca. 1900.

Federal Bureau of Prisons

Federal Bureau of Prisons

Spartan cell at McNeil Island was typical of living conditions in prisons about 1900.

Interior of the McNeil Island cellhouse.

Federal Bureau of Prisons

Aerial photo of the United States Penitentiary at Leavenworth, ca. 1930, shows massive cellblocks flanking the administration building (center), with smaller cellblocks radiating out from the rotunda. Inmates manufactured shoes and brushes in the factories beyond the cellhouses. There was ample room for baseball and other outdoor recreational activities within the walls. Inmates grew vegetables and grazed beef cattle in the surrounding fields.

Federal Bureau of Prisons

Federal Bureau of Prisons

An inmate transport wagon from the United States Penitentiary at Leavenworth, ca. 1905.

The layout of United States Penitentiary at Leavenworth with the long and massive flanking cellblocks, was similar to that of many other penitentiaries built in the late nineteenth and early twentieth centuries.

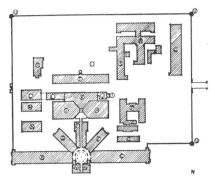

Federal Bureau of Prisons, *Handbook of Correctional Institution Design and Construction* (1949)

Federal Bureau of Prisons

Much of the food from the United States Penitentiary at Leavenworth's farms was consumed by inmates in the institution's main dining hall. Shown here about 1930, it looks like the stereotypical prison mess halls depicted in Hollywood gangster movies, with long benches, sullen inmates, and stern-looking officers.

Reform and Retribution: An Illustrated History of American Prisons

Prisons in Canada

Until the 1830s, there was very little prison development in Canada. In predominantly French-speaking Lower Canada (the English half of present-day Quebec and part of Newfoundland), and in English-speaking Upper Canada (the southern part of present-day Ontario), there was only a scattering of small, crudely built lockups. As was the case with prisons in Europe and the United States a half century earlier, classification of inmates was practically unknown. Debtors, convicted felons, suspects awaiting trial, and children in the care of incarcerated parents were intermingled in facilities that were little more than cabins. The vast territories of western Canada, meanwhile, were thinly populated and administered by the Hudson's Bay Company. A permanent jail for that region was first proposed in 1812, but was not established until 1835.

As alternatives to incarceration, both Upper and Lower Canada resorted to banishment, giving convicts a week or so to leave the province and never return; transportation to British penal colonies in Bermuda and Australia; and even branding. The stocks remained in use in Lower Canada until at least the 1830s, and the pillory in Upper Canada until the 1840s. Hudson's Bay Company officials in western Canada relied on fines for most violations, but transferred dangerous felons to authorities in Upper Canada or England. Further reducing the need for prison space was the fact that many petty crimes were punishable by death.

A prison reform movement got underway in Canada in the 1830s, as towns grew and crime increased. The most vocal proponent of reform was Charles Duncombe, who was a fervent advocate of installing moral reformation as the chief objective of imprisonment. In addition, officials of the provincial government in Upper Canada were impressed by advances being made by prisons in the United States. At the same time, Upper Canada was in the process of revising its criminal code, replacing execution with incarceration as the punishment for many crimes.

Because of Duncombe's urging, the influence of prisons in the United States, and the need for more prison space in light of the new criminal code, Canada's first penitentiary was established in Kingston, Ontario, in 1835. Initially serving Upper Canada exclusively, it began housing convicts from Lower Canada as well following the Act of Union in 1840.

Kingston Penitentiary was modeled on the New York State Penitentiary at Auburn. Auburn's Deputy Warden, William Powers, was recruited as deputy warden at Kingston, to advise Warden Henry Smith on Auburn's methods of prison management. Smith, who did not share authority gracefully, forced Powers out by 1840, and went on to rule Kingston Penitentiary with a firm and authoritarian hand. His regime was so brutal, tyrannical, corrupt, and inefficient, that it was condemned by a special governmental commission in 1849, and, the following year, Smith was removed from office.

Kingston Penitentiary, Canada's first, was opened in 1835.

Correctional Service of Canada

The Confederation of 1867 joined Upper and Lower Canada into a single country: the Dominion of Canada. The new federal government assumed control of Kingston Penitentiary and two other prisons. Under the Confederation, a two-tiered prison structure was established. First, the federal government operated prisons for offenders serving sentences of two years or more. Second, each of the provincial and territorial governments operated prisons for offenders serving less than two years. That basic structure has remained in place ever since, with the provincial and territorial corrections systems acquiring additional responsibilities for all juvenile offenders and probation cases.

One of the great figures of Canadian corrections of the nineteenth century was J. G. Moylan, who served as inspector of penitentiaries in the 1870s and 1880s. He presided over the opening of several new facilities, attacked corruption and inefficiency within the prison system, advocated improved living conditions for inmates, and emphasized the goal of reforming inmates—or, at least, ensuring that "none shall leave a prison a worse member of the community than when entering it."

If Kingston Penitentiary in the nineteenth century emulated New York's Auburn Prison, then Canadian correctional facilities in the twentieth century continued to reflect trends in the United States. By the 1930s and 1940s, the Penitentiary Service of Canada began housing inmates in open dormitories whenever appropriate (as was being done increasingly in the United States), upgraded classification procedures, and diversified its institutions to make classification more effective. In 1947, the Canadian Department of Justice announced a "new deal" for inmates—including improvements in counseling and casework, structured leisure time activities, and other innovations designed to help rehabilitate offenders—that resembled the "individualized treatment" programs that prison systems in the United States had begun implementing in the 1920s and 1930s. Staff training also was improved, with a centralized training system introduced in 1948, and a Penitentiary Staff College established in 1952.

Canadian Parks Service

Bordeaux provincial jail, near Montreal, Canada, built between 1908 and 1913.

By the 1990s, Canada seemed to be embracing another fashion from the United States: the trend toward longer sentences and harder time. Longer sentences were mandated for certain high-risk offenders, mandatory minimum sentences were imposed, parole revocations increased, and Canada's rate of incarceration reached levels that were quite high in comparison with most countries other than the United States. Nevertheless, Canada remained committed to "doing good corrections," in the words of Ole Ingstrup, Commissioner of the Correctional Service of Canada for two separate terms in the 1980s and 1990s. Canada emphasized alternative sanctions whenever feasible, such as probation, and reasserted its commitment to rehabilitative programming.

In 1977, following a series of disturbances and other violent activities in Canadian prisons, a Parliamentary committee declared that Canadian corrections was in a "state of crisis," and ordered a broad review of prison management. The review led to a new philosophical orientation for the Canadian prison system. Under Ingstrup and his predecessor, Donald Yeomans, the Correctional Service of Canada adopted a new mission statement in the 1980s that made the reintegration of offenders into the community a central objective. Recognizing that the "offender has the potential to live as a law-abiding citizen," the mission statement held that the Correctional Service of Canada accepted as one of its primary responsibilities the task of providing offenders with the tools they would need to change their criminal lifestyles.

National Prison Congress
Declaration of Principles

The first National Prison Congress, meeting in Cincinnati in 1870, adopted a Declaration of Principles, which is summarized below. It remains a progressive document of correctional goals. The Declaration advocated:

1. Establishing reformation, not vindictive suffering, as the purpose of penal treatment

2. Making classifications on the basis of a mark system, patterned after the Irish system

3. Rewarding good conduct

4. Helping prisoners realize that their destiny is in their own hands

5. Removing the chief obstacles to prison reform, namely: the political appointment of prison officials and the instability of management

6. Providing job training for prison officials

7. Replacing fixed sentences with indeterminate sentences; removing the gross disparities and inequities in prison sentences and demonstrating the futility of repeated short sentences

8. Establishing religion and education as the most important agencies of reformation

9. Using prison discipline that gained the will of prisoners and conserved their self-respect

10. Making industrious freemen rather than orderly and obedient prisoners as prison's aim

11. Urging full provision for industrial training

12. Abolishing the system of contract labor in prison

13. Establishing small prisons and separate institutions for different types of offenders

14. Laws striking against the so-called "higher-ups" in crime, as well as against the lesser operatives

15. Indemnifying prisoners who later were discovered to be innocent

16. Revising laws relating to the treatment of insane criminals

17. Making more judicious exercise of pardoning power

18. Establishing a system for the collection of uniform penal statistics

19. Developing more adequate prison architecture, providing sufficiently for air and sunlight, as well as for prison hospitals, schoolrooms, and such

20. Establishing central prison management within each state

21. Facilitating the social training of prisoners through proper associations and abolishing the silence rule

22. Making society at large realize its responsibility for crime conditions

23. "In the official administration of such a [prison] system and in the voluntary cooperation of citizens, therein, the agency of women may be employed with excellent effect."

5

New Century, New Directions

New York Department of Corrections

Most aspects of the theoretical basis for modern prisons were in place by 1900, at least in embryonic form. Incarceration—not whipping, beating, or executing criminals—should be the primary form of punishment for convicted felons; offenders should undergo a process of reform or rehabilitation while in prison, and they should not be degraded or exploited; and prisons should be clean, safe, and managed by professionals.

It was not an easy task, however, to move from theories to practice. Some prisons, under the leadership of competent and well-intentioned wardens, did strive to attain the standards put forth by the National Prison Association and various prison reform groups, such as the John Howard Society, the Women's Prison Association of New York, and the Thomas Mott Osborne Society.

Yet, most state prisons and county jails remained cramped, filthy, dispiriting places. Conditions for female inmates were particularly atrocious. And the controversy over prison labor was becoming increasingly vexatious. During the first quarter of the twentieth century, notable progress was made toward implementing some of the bold theories developed during the last quarter of the nineteenth century.

American Correctional Association

Inmates in large state prisons during the 1900s, such as those marching in the main yard at Auburn Penitentiary (above), had greater likelihood of finding comparatively humane conditions than the miserable guests of county jails and city lockups (bottom), where accommodations frequently were horrendous.

Inmates from Folsom State Prison in California work a rock quarry in Represa.

California Department of Corrections

Joliet inmates toil in a prison factory under the contract system, ca. 1900.

Federal Bureau of Prisons

Reform and Retribution: An Illustrated History of American Prisons

The State-use System

Historically, there have been four reasons for making inmates work: (1) to raise revenue to help cover prison operating expenses; (2) to make punishment more onerous through the assignment of such exhausting, pointless, and monotonous tasks as breaking up rocks, powering treadmills, or moving heavy cannon balls from one corner of the prison yard to another, and then back again; (3) to provide job training that could further an inmate's rehabilitation; and (4) to manage the inmates more effectively by keeping them busy and out of mischief.

During the nineteenth century, the first two motivations were paramount: raising revenue and increasing the pain of incarceration. That changed during the first part of the twentieth century, and the emphasis was placed on prison labor as a management tool and a rehabilitative strategy.

State prisons in the nineteenth century could generate revenue through inmate labor in one of three ways: either by having inmates produce goods in prison-operated factories or farms, and then selling those goods on the open market (public account system); by accepting payment from contractors to put state prisoners to work in privately run factories in or near the prison (contract system); or by actually leasing prisoners to contractors who not only put them to work but were responsible for incarcerating them (convict leasing system).

Factory at unidentified prison produced clothing for inmates, early 1900s.

American Correctional Association

Many in business and organized labor deemed all three systems to be detrimental to private enterprise and free labor. Critics feared that goods produced by prison labor would be sold well below market price, undercut products produced by companies that did not employ prisoners, and drive down the wages of noninmate labor.

Business had long protested against the unfair competition from the products of inmate labor. By the 1890s, for the first time, labor unions were gaining the stability and strength to have a voice in politics, and they also were opposed to selling prison-produced merchandise on the open market.

Moved by arguments that prison-made goods hurt business and labor—and, to a lesser extent, by the observation that convict leasing and contracting were brutal and exploitative—several state governments during the last quarter of the nineteenth century prohibited the leasing or contracting of inmate labor, and also prohibited production by inmates of goods for sale to the public. New Jersey, Pennsylvania, and New York were among the first states to enact such laws, and, in 1887, the United States Congress prohibited the leasing of federal inmates.

Baking loaves of bread for prison mess tables at the United States Penitentiary at McNeil Island about 1907 was one of the few inmate jobs that did not create some type of controversy.

Federal Bureau of Prisons

Reform and Retribution: An Illustrated History of American Prisons

Illinois Department of Corrections

Prison labor, early 1900s: blacksmith shop at Illinois State Penitentiary, Pontiac, and shed for cinder blocks, Riker's Island, New York.

New York Department of Corrections

New Century, New Directions

Indiana Department of Corrections

California Department of Corrections

Reform and Retribution: An Illustrated History of American Prisons

Indiana Department of Corrections

By the 1930s, inmate labor included foundry work (opposite top) and broom-making (above) at the Indiana Reformatory in Pendleton, as well as work in the tailor shop at Folsom Prison in California (opposite bottom).

More states prohibited or restricted productive labor by inmates during the early twentieth century. In 1929, 1935, and 1940, federal laws were enacted that prohibited interstate commerce in prison-made goods.

Clamping down on the production and retail sale of prison-made goods, however, led to another problem: inmate idleness. With no work to do in prison factories, except to produce inmate uniforms, chairs, cots, and other goods that would be used within the prison, the only assignments left were those needed to keep prisons functioning, such as performing janitorial work, painting, doing general repairs, groundskeeping, and preparing food. There was not enough work to do around prisons to keep everyone busy. One Ohio warden was so desperate for work assignments to occupy inmates that he ordered one inmate to spend his entire day keeping salt and pepper shakers on mess hall tables neatly lined up.

Days, weeks, and years of enforced idleness for inmates threatened prison stability. Idleness not only gave inmates more time to concentrate on escape plans and other illicit activities, it also gave rise to great boredom and frustration among the inmates— which in turn led to heightened tension and increased violence by inmates against other inmates and against prison staff.

In an effort to keep inmates occupied without having a deleterious effect on the free market, state prisons began turning to the state-use system exclusively. Under the state-use system, inmates could produce goods, but those goods could not be sold on the open market. Instead, they could be sold only to government agencies in the state where the prison was located.

By the 1920s, nearly a dozen states restricted inmate labor to the state-use system. The most famous example of products manufactured in prison factories under the state-use system were license plates for automobiles, but other examples included printed materials, shoes, brushes, clothing, towels, bricks, and office furniture.

Pioneers in the state-use system included New York, Ohio, Pennsylvania, and New Jersey. In 1919, federal prisons began producing goods under the state-use system for sale to United States government agencies; Leavenworth Penitentiary, for example, made shoes, and Atlanta Penitentiary produced textile goods—most of which were sold to the Army, Navy, and Veterans Administration. Further refinements were introduced in federal prisons in 1935 with the establishment of Federal Prison Industries, Incorporated.

The prison factory in Angola, Louisiana, ca. 1930, manufactured prison license plates.

Louisiana Department of Corrections

Shoe factory, the United States Penitentiary at Leavenworth, ca. 1919.

Federal Bureau of Prisons

Two other types of inmate employment covered by the state-use system were road building and farming. In many of the states, inmates constructed and maintained public highways. Inmates were housed in barracks or tents known as road camps. Accommodations in the early road camps were substandard in many ways. In addition, road camps—particularly in the South—were associated with the notorious chain gangs that became a national scandal by the 1930s. Yet, the road camps were the predecessors of the youth camps, honor camps, and minimum-security camps that appeared in the 1930s and 1940s, and which continue to be a very positive element in America's prison systems.

In the early 1900s, state inmates worked as "gandy dancers," building and repairing railroads.

American Correctional Association

Inmates from California state prisons helped build the Yosemite Highway, ca. 1920.

California Department of Corrections

Forestry and roadwork meant tent camps and honor camps for inmates requiring less security (opposite and below); road work could also mean chain gangs (opposite, below left). (Opposite, below right) Bunk room of prison road camp, early twentieth century.

American Correctional Association

Reform and Retribution: An Illustrated History of American Prisons

American Correctional Association

American Correctional Association

American Correctional Association

In the early twentieth century, many states continued to lease inmates to work in agricultural operations. In addition, some prison-owned farms produced flax, cotton, fruit, and vegetables for public sale, but farms could readily be adapted to the state-use system.

Prison dairy farms, cattle herds, piggeries, vegetable gardens, and fruit orchards produced food for use within the prison. As an offshoot of the farming operations, slaughterhouses, canneries, and other food processing operations were maintained behind prison walls. Federal prisons exchanged products—beef from Leavenworth Penitentiary, for example, could be traded for apples from McNeil Island Penitentiary. Federal prisons also sold dairy products to the military.

American Correctional Association

For most of the twentieth century—until small-scale farming became too costly and food could be purchased less expensively from suppliers—prison farms were very common. Pictured, inmates going to work and a work detail in the fields at the Indiana State Prison, ca. 1915.

American Correctional Association

Reform and Retribution: An Illustrated History of American Prisons

Not only did employment of inmates in prison factories and on prison farms alleviate idleness and improve prison management, it also taught inmates valuable job skills and work habits. That aspect of inmate labor would be emphasized more explicitly in the 1930s, when the concept of "individualized treatment" began coming into vogue.

Federal Bureau of Prisons

Farming operations at the United States Penitentiary at Leavenworth, ca. 1950.

Inmates in urban areas worked at local tasks. Garbage scow docked at Riker's Island Prison, New York, ready for inmates to unload it and separate out wood and other usable refuse (1924).

New York Department of Corrections

Shipbuilding and logging at the United
States Penitentiary at McNeil Island,
ca. 1900.

Federal Bureau of Prisons

Federal Bureau of Prisons

Reform and Retribution: An Illustrated History of American Prisons

New Prison Technologies and Living Conditions

Many prisons began to implement a variety of technological innovations in the first years of the twentieth century. Some new technologies improved prison security—and, in so doing, improved prison living conditions by enhancing safety. Some technologies were intended primarily to improve living conditions, but they also had desirable security implications.

Strap-iron, latticework doors at Washington State Penitentiary were typical of cells built at the turn of the century.

Washington Department of Corrections

Bertillon identification card for John Arnold, a member of the notorious Butch Cassidy Gang, who was an inmate at the United States Penitentiary at Atlanta in the early 1900s.

Federal Bureau of Prisons, Reprinted from *Corrections Today*, July 1995

A major technological shift occurred at the turn of the century in the area of inmate identification: fingerprinting replaced the Bertillon System. The Bertillon System was an identification process developed in 1873 for the French police, and it was in common use in American prisons by the 1880s.

Using calipers, sliding compasses, and other instruments, Bertillon operators took measurements of inmates' skulls, fingers, arms, and feet; classified the shape of inmates' noses; described scars and marks; and noted other characteristics to ensure positive identification. Not to be confused with phrenology or Cesare Lombroso's theories of skull shapes as indicators of character traits, the Bertillon System measured physical attributes—such as head width—that would not change over time in a mature adult. Bertillon measurements often were considered by prison officials to be more reliable than the photographs of inmates that sometimes accompanied them.

Fingerprinting, which developed in England, was almost as old as the Bertillon System. It was not generally accepted in American prisons, however, until its superiority to the Bertillon System was demonstrated dramatically in 1903. Will West, an inmate at

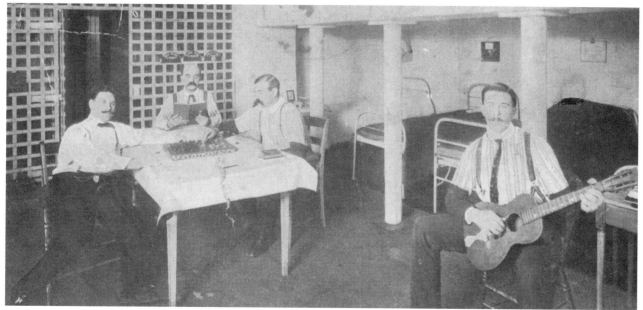

Ohio State Penitentiary

Staff members at Ohio State Penitentiary in Columbus taking a break (above); behind them is a latticework grille—which was much less secure than the case-hardened, cylindrical bars (below).

Leavenworth Penitentiary, was nearly mistaken for another inmate, William West, who bore a strong facial resemblance to him, was of the same height, weight, and age, and had identical Bertillon measurements. They could be distinguished only by their fingerprints. As a result, fingerprinting rapidly replaced Bertillon measurements in American prisons.

Another important advance was in cell-door technology. For most of the nineteenth century, cell doors typically were hung on hinges and were constructed of flat straps of iron that were interlaced in a latticework pattern. Although this type of door was still being installed after 1900, some prisons were moving to a more secure type of cell door. Those doors slid on tracks, were operated mechanically from a single point on the tier, and were constructed of cylindrical, case-hardened, tool-resistant steel bars. The brand new federal penitentiaries at Atlanta (1902) and Leavenworth (1906) featured this new type of door, which became the standard for twentieth century prisons.

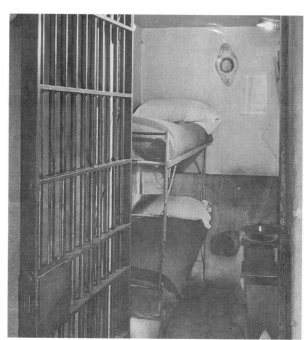

American Correctional Association

New York Department of Corrections

Centrally operated, sliding grille doors, at Attica (New York) State Prison, 1954.

Hinged, individually padlocked cell doors at Chicago House of Correction.

Corrections Today

Early version of centralized locking apparatus, at Sing Sing Prison (New York). Device at top of cells controlled swinging grille doors from a central location at the end of the tier. Later, centrally controlled cell doors slid on tracks, making them less vulnerable to tampering.

Corrections Today/David Kemmerling

Federal Bureau of Prisons, *Handbook of Correctional Institution Design and Construction* (1949)

Electrically operated grille doors (note instrument panel on left), United States Penitentiary at Alcatraz, ca. 1940.

Federal Bureau of Prisons, *Handbook of Correctional Institution Design and Construction* (1949)

Manually operated grille doors (note levers at right), United States Penitentiary, Alcatraz, ca. 1940.

There was never any shortage of clever ideas about how to control or restrain inmates. In addition to the usual selection of handcuffs, shackles, and leg irons, there were such hobbles as balls and chains, as well as the notorious Oregon Boot—footwear fitted with a metal ring over the ankle to make running impossible. Clubs, thumb-screws, the pillory, and the whipping post were also still in evidence at the beginning of the twentieth century. However, according to the Rev. William C. Stoudenmire of the Maryland Prisoners' Aid Association, by 1902 some of those devices were "going out of use."

New York Department of Corrections

Inmates at Sing Sing (New York), 1916, shackled in leg irons that were five-feet long and weighed twenty-pounds each.

Reform and Retribution: An Illustrated History of American Prisons

Ed Clark, *Life Magazine*, 1943

Hobbled inmate looks surprisingly serene. Iron "picks," riveted above his ankles, make running impossible. Burlap wrappings underneath the picks prevented chafing.

Attire aided in inmate identification. Right, Joliet inmates in stripes at a turn-of-the-century Fourth of July ceremony are more readily identifiable as prisoners. Auburn prisoners (also at an Independence Day celebration) may have been less readily identifiable.

American Correctional Association

Reform and Retribution: An Illustrated History of American Prisons

Illinois Department of Corrections

Steel box provided added security, as well as added misery for prisoners inside it.

American Correctional Association

Electric chair and accompanying apparatus, Ohio State Penitentiary, ca. 1900.

Ohio Department of Correction

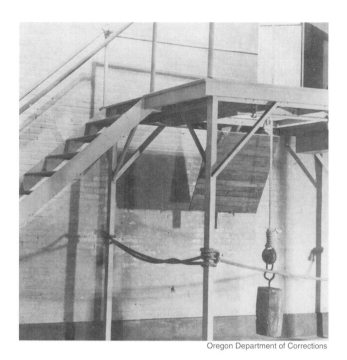

Oregon Department of Corrections

Undoubtedly the grimmest advance in prison technology was the electric chair. Although the number of capital crimes had diminished severely since the eighteenth century, murder, rape, and a few other offenses remained punishable by death in many states. Hanging was the preferred method in the nineteenth century, and some states used firing squads, but death by electrocution was widely considered the most humane and efficient method in the early 1900s.

Capital punishment technology: scaffold at Oregon State Penitentiary; electric chair at Ohio State Penitentiary in Columbus.

Corrections Today

Technological innovations also made improvements in prison living conditions possible. New prisons, such as the penitentiaries at Atlanta and Leavenworth, were built with plumbing, electric lighting, steam heat, and, for official use by staff, telephones. Those modern conveniences were appearing in homes and workplaces throughout the United States around 1900, but they had added value in prison settings.

Modern, in-cell plumbing not only meant better sanitation but also fewer security risks associated with opening cell doors to remove night buckets (or "honey pots"), or maintaining rudimentary forms of plumbing that gave inmates opportunities to communicate surreptitiously by tapping on pipes. Electricity, meanwhile, provided illumination that was safer than gas lamps and also provided brighter and more efficient lighting, thereby improving security. More generally, better sanitation, warmer cellblocks, and improved lighting undoubtedly contributed to greater stability by enhancing physical comfort for staff and inmates alike and reducing tension.

Just because technologies were available, however, does not mean that they were universally adopted. Night buckets, poor lighting, and other undesirable remnants of nineteenth-century prisons prevailed in many institutions well into the twentieth century. After 1900, however, an increasing number of prisons were installing modern conveniences, with obvious benefits for security and stability.

In 1924, inmates line up to empty "honey pots" into sewer trough; a twice daily procedure at the Welfare Island Penitentiary in New York.

American Correctional Association

Federal Bureau of Prisons

Better medical care for inmates and improved sanitation have been hallmarks of prison reform efforts. Sometimes denounced as inmate coddling, healthier prisons actually are safer and more secure. Pictured: physician at Atlanta penitentiary, 1906; sanitation inspector surveying a state prison in Massachusetts, ca. 1920.

Massachusetts Department of Corrections

Prisons for Women

Prisons for women also underwent improvements during the early twentieth century. They certainly needed it. As unsatisfactory as prison conditions may have been for men in the nineteenth century, they were far worse for women. Typically, female prisoners were relegated to the basements, attics, and corners of male prisons, were subjected to degrading treatment, and were under the supervision of male guards.

The great English prison reformer Elizabeth Fry (1780-1845) had found similar conditions in the early nineteenth century at London's Newgate Prison. She called for separate prisons for women that would feature rehabilitative vocational, educational, and religious training. She also insisted that women's prisons be administered by women.

Munro, *The New York Tombs Inside and Out* (1909)

Women's section, Tombs Prison, New York City, in the late nineteenth century.

New York Department of Corrections

The Women's Prison at Auburn, New York, was opened on May 29, 1893.

Eliza W. B. Farnham introduced important reforms when she served as head matron at the women's section of Sing Sing Prison.

New York Historical Society

Fry's proposals were championed by prison reformers in the United States who sought to improve conditions for female inmates. Early efforts to implement them included the opening of a separate building for female juvenile offenders at the New York City House of Refuge in 1825. From 1844 to 1848, Eliza W. B. Farnham (1815-1864) was head matron of the women's section at Sing Sing Prison in Ossining, New York. She stressed rehabilitative programming and tried to create an atmosphere for the women that was more like the idealized middle-class home and less like prison.

Private and religious societies also attempted to assist female offenders. In New York City, the Women's Prison Association and the Hopper House established institutions for female offenders that were forerunners of the modern halfway house. Those institutions provided religious guidance, vocational instruction, and medical care, and they were staffed by women. They preceded by many years similar efforts for male offenders.

New York Department of Corrections

Kitchen of Auburn Women's Prison, ca. 1900.

Ensuring that female inmates were supervised by female staff was an essential element of the effort to reform women's prisons. Apart from the obvious fears that female inmates might be vulnerable to physical abuse from male guards, there were two reasons for this.

First was the conviction that men were an important part of the environment that led women to break the law. To become reformed, it was believed that those women needed to be incarcerated in a more wholesome and nurturing environment—one that, almost by definition, excluded men.

Illinois Department of Corrections

Cleaning detail, women's section at Joliet (Illinois) Prison, early 1900s.

Reform and Retribution: An Illustrated History of American Prisons

The second reason was that proponents of prisons run by and for women believed that the problems that led to a woman becoming a criminal could be understood only by other women. In her report to the 1898 National Prison Congress, the Superintendent of the Massachusetts Reformatory for Women, Ellen Johnson, stated that "none but a woman" could understand the "mental vagaries" of women with "distressed bodies and unstrung nerves" that were "the legitimate result of a life of sin."

Some advances were made during the Reformatory Era of the late nineteenth century. Reformatories for women were set up in Indiana (1873), Massachusetts (1877), and New York (1887 and 1893). In general, however, conditions were little changed for female offenders since the 1830s and 1840s, when famed asylum reformer Dorothea Dix (1802-1887) urged removing women from male-administered state prisons, and when Chaplain B.C. Smith of Auburn Penitentiary lamented that women in prison suffered fates "worse than death."

Ward in Auburn Women's Prison, ca. 1900.

New York Department of Corrections

Special housing unit for disciplinary cases, Bedford Hills Reformatory for Women, New York, 1906.

New York Department of Corrections

Female federal offenders, for example, sometimes were housed in improvised quarters in the male penitentiaries at Leavenworth and McNeil Island, or boarded at state prisons for men in Columbus, Ohio and Moundsville, West Virginia. After visiting the Columbus and Moundsville facilities, Justice Department official Judith Ellen Foster (1840-1910) reported in 1908 that "present conditions [for female inmates] ought not to continue" because they were "useless for good and terrible for evil human beings." She even found evidence of corporal punishment being inflicted on female prisoners. Foster's reports received serious attention in Washington, but a planned facility at Leavenworth to house female prisoners exclusively failed to materialize.

Massachusetts Department of Corrections

Work assignments at women's prisons in the early 1900s were varied, and they were focused on supporting prison operations. Inmates make bread at the Sherborn (Massachusetts) Reformatory for Women, and iron clothes at an unidentified facility.

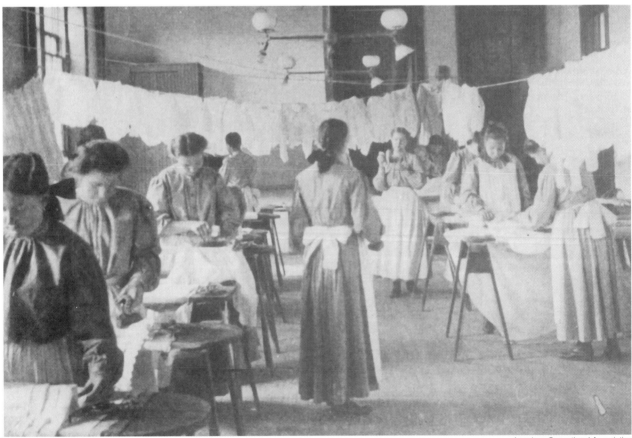

American Correctional Association

Reform and Retribution: An Illustrated History of American Prisons

During the early 1900s, the Progressive Era gave rise to political reforms and helped establish a national mood that was more conducive to improving prisons for women. An important part of the Progressive movement was suffragism and increased political activism on the part of women. As women became more involved in political activities and civic organizations, they began to press for better prisons for female offenders.

New York Department of Corrections

Work assignments for female inmates also included baling hay at the Bedford Hills (New York) Reformatory for Women, and building a water tower at Bedford Hills.

New York Department of Corrections

Some of the suffragettes and other women reformers experienced the deplorable prison conditions firsthand, when they were jailed for civil disobedience around the time of World War I. The public exposure that those women gave to prison conditions helped bring about change. Among the most eloquent protests from jailed women were lodged by radicals, such as the anarchist Emma Goldman (1869-1940) and the socialist Kate Richards O'Hare (1877-1948). Much more influential, however, were upper class and professional women incarcerated for such activities as picketing the White House on behalf of women's suffrage. Working through such establishment organizations as the General Federation of Women's Clubs and the Women's Christian Temperance Union, they influenced lawmakers and shaped public opinion on the subject of women's prisons.

New reformatories for women inmates were opened in Bedford Hills, New York (1901), Clinton, New Jersey (1913), and elsewhere. And, due in no small measure to intensive lobbying by the General Federation of Women's Clubs, the federal government opened its first reformatory for women in Alderson, West Virginia (1927).

Because the number of female prisoners was minuscule in comparison with the number of male prisoners, the resources devoted to women's prisons were not great. At the same time, because female prisoners were considered less dangerous than male prisoners, administrators of the new women's reformatories were given considerable latitude in programming. As a result, they developed an array of prison innovations—many of which ultimately became standard even in men's prisons.

Nurseries have not been uncommon in women's prisons. Infants born to incarcerated mothers typically remained with their mothers—in the prison—until they were several months old. Some children, especially if no family members or foster homes were able to take them, remained in prison nurseries until they were toddlers. Pictured is the nursery at the Connecticut State Farm and Prison for Women, ca. 1950.

Connecticut Department of Corrections

Reform and Retribution: An Illustrated History of American Prisons

Katherine B. Davis (1860-1935), as the first superintendent of the Bedford Hills Reformatory for Women, brought in physicians, psychologists, and psychiatrists to help classify prisoners by behavior and to develop treatment programs for them—a harbinger of the "Medical Model" that would emerge as a major theme in American corrections decades later. Many of the new reformatories featured decentralized complexes of cottages or dormitories instead of massive cellblocks, enhanced education classes, libraries, art and musical programs, recreational opportunities, work release, and even inmate councils (for limited inmate self-government)—all of which appeared later in men's prisons. Clearly, Davis and others who administered women's prisons developed and implemented programs that gave rise to important trends in corrections, such as individualized treatment (see Chapter 6).

Women's prisons pioneered in the development of housing for prisoners that was more humane and less restrictive. Cottages or dormitories replaced traditional cellblocks, attempted to replicate middle-class domesticity, and presaged modern unit management and modular housing. Pictured are cottages at the Federal Women's Reformatory in Alderson, West Virginia (ca. 1929) and the Industrial School for Girls in Bon Air, Virginia (1939).

Federal Bureau of Prisons

Virginia Department of Corrections

Federal Bureau of Prisons

Warden Mary Harris promoted industrial programs for women at Alderson (top photo this page), as well as home economics (bottom), and farming (top, opposite page).

Federal Bureau of Prisons

Federal Bureau of Prisons

Reform and Retribution: An Illustrated History of American Prisons

Federal Bureau of Prisons

Innovative women's prisons in the early and mid-twentieth century encouraged a more home-like setting; cells such as those at the Federal Women's Reformatory in Alderson in the 1940s contained many personal effects and resembled the bedrooms of college dormitories.

Federal Bureau of Prisons

Inmates work on the farm at the Industrial School for Girls, Bon Air, Virginia (1939).

Virginia Department of Corrections

Willebrandt and Harris

Although the public generally assumes that corrections is a male-dominated profession, women have made profound contributions to the field. In the nineteenth century, Dorothea Dix (1802-1887) challenged the nation to improve conditions for all institutionalized people, whether in prisons, insane asylums, or poorhouses. While best known for her work with the mentally ill, her efforts on behalf of prisoners brought about many improvements in prison conditions. Her book, *Remarks on Prisons and Prison Discipline in the United States* (1845) exposed substandard conditions and made proposals for reforms that would be adopted many decades later.

In the early twentieth century, J. Ellen Foster (1840-1910), as an official with the U.S. Justice Department, initiated significant improvements in the treatment of female federal offenders. About the same time, Katherine B. Davis was introducing important new penological concepts, including the psychiatric assessment of inmates, at the Bedford Hills facility in New York. Davis eventually became Commissioner of Corrections in New York City.

Following in the tradition of Dix, Foster, and Davis were Mabel Walker Willebrandt (1889-1963) and Mary Belle Harris (1874-1957). From 1924 to 1929, Willebrandt was Assistant Attorney General of the United States in charge of matters relating to prisons, taxation, and prohibition. She later moved to Hollywood and served for many years as General Counsel of the Screen Actors Guild. A Quaker, like many prison reformers of earlier generations, Willebrandt was in many respects the founder of the Federal Bureau of Prisons. Having already established a federal reformatory for male juveniles in Chillicothe, Ohio, and one for women in Alderson, West Virginia, Willebrandt hired Sanford Bates in 1929 as Superintendent of Prisons. Her instructions to Bates, even before he was sworn in, were to work with her in pushing through Congress legislation that would centralize and improve federal prison operations by establishing the Federal Bureau of Prisons.

Mabel Walker Willebrandt, Assistant Attorney General of the United States (1921-1929).

Federal Bureau of Prisons

Three years earlier, Willebrandt hired Mary Belle Harris to be the first warden of the Alderson facility. A professor of ancient philology at Bryn Mawr College with a doctorate in Sanskrit from the University of Chicago, Harris had become involved in social work at Chicago's famous Hull House. Drawn into corrections by Katherine Davis, Harris built an excellent reputation as an administrator of women's prisons and detention facilities for girls in New York and New Jersey, and with the U.S. War Department. At Alderson, she developed a campus-like setting and introduced classification, as well as work and education programs, all of which ultimately were adopted by male prisons.

Not only are more women employed in the 1990s as line staff in prisons, from correctional officers, to teachers, to psychologists, but there are an increasing number of women in the top ranks, like Harris and Willebrandt. In 1992, Kathleen M. Hawk was appointed Director of the Federal Bureau of Prisons. She was just one of several women in charge of corrections systems during the 1990s; others included Margaret Moore in the District of Columbia, Sally Chandler Halford in Iowa, Peggy Wallace in Kentucky, Dora Schriro in Missouri, Judith Uphoff in Wyoming, and Elaine Little in North Dakota.

Federal Bureau of Prisons

First Lady Eleanor Roosevelt (left) visited Warden Mary B. Harris at the Federal Women's Reformatory at Alderson in 1934. Mrs. Roosevelt took a strong interest in Alderson and corrections programs for women.

Federal Bureau of Prisons Director Kathleen M. Hawk, at her swearing-in ceremony in 1992, flanked by predecessors J. Michael Quinlan (left) and Norman A. Carlson (right).

Federal Bureau of Prisons

6

The Goal of Individualized Treatment

The various approaches to corrections that had been evolving since the early 1800s—prison as a place of punishment but also as a place of reform, prison as a humane environment, classification of inmates, corrections work as a profession instead of a dumping ground for political appointees—converged by the 1920s and 1930s with an emphasis on "individualized treatment" based on "scientific penology."

Federal Bureau of Prisons

James V. Bennett (1894-1978), Director of the Federal Bureau of Prisons from 1937 to 1964, disliked the word "penology" because he thought it reflected a "naive" attempt to "reduce to a science the unhappy task of punishing people." Yet, Bennett was one of the strongest and ablest proponents of the movement to professionalize prison services and to develop treatment plans for each offender based on scientific observations and precepts. That movement produced wide-reaching changes in prison settings and prison activities, and prepared the way for the so-called "Medical Model" of a later generation, in which the goal of rehabilitation would be paramount.

Vocational training in airplane mechanics prepared inmates at Chillicothe Youth Reformatory for employment in defense factories after release during World War II.

Scientific Penology

In the early and mid-twentieth century, criminologists, social scientists, social workers, and prison administrators applied theories from the emerging fields of sociology, psychology, and psychiatry to study crime and punishment, and to attempt to create a more beneficial prison environment. Around 1910, university professors and clinical psychologists began establishing research centers connected with courts or prisons to collect and analyze data on offenders.

The Laboratory of Social Hygiene was established at Bedford Hills Women's Reformatory in New York in 1912 to study the psychology of female offenders. In 1916, Dr. Bernard Glueck set up a clinic at New York's Sing Sing Prison to examine each incoming inmate. By the 1920s, Harvard and nearly a dozen other universities and law schools had developed courses on criminal psychology that further fueled the proliferation of clinics and institutes to study criminal behavior and sanctions.

Business mathematics class at the National Training School for Boys, near Washington, D.C., late 1940s.

Federal Bureau of Prisons

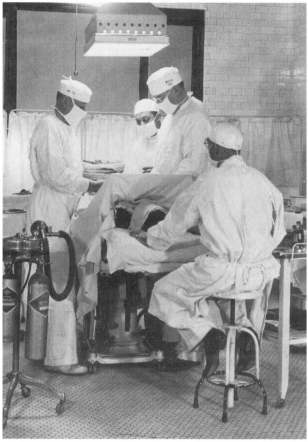

New York Department of Corrections

The findings and recommendations of these clinics influenced such groups as the National Crime Commission and the National Commission on Law Observance and Enforcement (popularly known as the Wickersham Commission). In the late 1920s and early 1930s, those groups urged better classification of inmates, progressive treatment to "reshape" inmates into law-abiding members of society, and the maintenance of a suitably uplifting environment in prison that would help achieve those goals, along lines suggested by the burgeoning research on prisons and prisoners.

Conditions of confinement improved significantly from the 1920s through the 1940s. Operating room at Sing Sing Prison, New York (early 1930s), shows higher standards in medical treatment for inmates. The four-inmate cell at the United States Penitentiary at Leavenworth (ca. 1935) is clean, well-lit, has plumbing, and features lockers for inmates to store personal property.

Federal Bureau of Prisons

Prison cell, 1939.

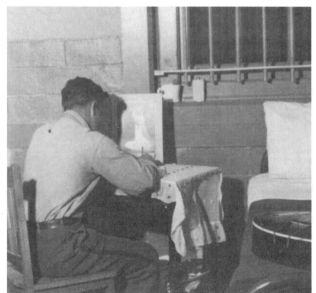

American Correctional Association

In essence, the clinics, social scientists, and crime commissions were calling for a renewal of the old reformatory concept, but with much greater sophistication. Whereas classification during the Reformatory Era was rudimentary, superficial, and used primarily for maintaining internal discipline, classification as a component of scientific penology would be based on clinical evidence. The focus would be on developing individualized treatment programs that took into account the social and criminal histories of offenders, their personalities, and their unique needs and which would be geared to preparing inmates for release.

Individualized treatment would include many of the same elements as the old reformatories—education classes, libraries, vocational training—but there would be a greater commitment to them; efforts to make those programs work would be redoubled.

Classification—to determine each inmate's appropriate security level, housing, job assignment, education program, and so on—was an important element of individualized treatment. Institution classification committees typically included the warden, captain, chief medical officer, chief psychologist, chaplain, and supervisor of education. Here, a classification committee at the New Jersey State Prison in Trenton (early 1930s) reviews an inmate's file.

New Jersey Department of Corrections

Inmates pass through primitive metal detector at the United States Penitentiary at McNeil Island, 1935.

Federal Bureau of Prisons

Reform and Retribution: An Illustrated History of American Prisons

Individualized treatment also would mean customized prison settings. Different classifications in the early reformatories involved little more than giving inmates different sorts of work assignments and different levels of privileges—but all within the same prison. The newer approach, however, called for different types of prisons that would focus on the needs of certain categories of offenders. Instead of all offenders being grouped together, no matter what their grade or classification, they would be housed, as appropriate, in minimum-security camps, medium-security facilities, narcotics farms, psychiatric hospitals, or whatever type of facility could provide the environment and treatment program that they warranted. Only the most hard-core, intractable, and dangerous inmates would be confined in the maximum-security penitentiaries that previously had been the sort of prison where the vast majority of inmates were housed. There was an economic advantage to that approach as well. Typical maximum-security penitentiaries—with the heavy security, the high walls, the added grilles and locks—were more expensive to build and operate than lower-security facilities. Classification and diversified housing would be limited to those inmates who required added security.

Inmate meets with warden and other members of classification committee at the United States Penitentiary at Atlanta, ca. 1948.

Federal Bureau of Prisons

Inmate appears before New York State Parole Board, Sing Sing Prison, ca. 1935. A widely held principle of individualized treatment was that inmates should be released before their sentences expired, if they responded well to their rehabilitation programs. More pragmatically, early release was one of the very few tools that prison officials could use to induce good behavior and prevent misconduct.

New York Department of Corrections

Federal Bureau of Prisons

Graduated security levels even had an impact on visiting procedures. Restrictions remained tight at high-security penitentiaries (below) in the 1940s, but were greatly reduced at medium and low-security facilities (above).

Federal Bureau of Prisons

American Correctional Association

Austin MacCormick was a leading exponent of individualized treatment. He served as New York City's Commissioner of Corrections, Assistant Director of the Federal Bureau of Prisons, and President of the American Correctional Association.

As with the best intentions and highest ideals of the separate system, the congregate system, and the reformatory system, the aims of scientific penology were difficult to achieve in practice. Many prison systems, of course, did not even try. Thoroughly wretched conditions continued to prevail in many parts of the country. County jails in the South during the 1930s, for instance, may have been as inhumane as anything in the eighteenth century.

Yet, there were prison administrators who worked diligently to carry out new objectives. In New York, Austin MacCormick (1893-1979) devised state-of-the-art education and treatment programs. In the New Jersey prison system, F. Lovell Bixby did pathbreaking work in the area of classification.

After 1930, however, a new corrections agency took the lead in promoting the concept of scientific penology and individualized treatment. After 150 years of playing either a secondary role or no role at all in the field, the federal government finally moved into the forefront of corrections with the creation of the Federal Bureau of Prisons.

Federal deputy marshals escort new prisoner to the Federal Bureau of Prisons facility in Springfield, Missouri, late 1930s.

Federal Bureau of Prisons

The Federal Bureau of Prisons

The federal penitentiaries established by the Three Prisons Act of 1891 quickly proved inadequate to the task of housing the increasing number of federal offenders. Three new federal laws, in particular, helped to swell the federal inmate population beyond a reasonable point: the Volstead Act (prohibiting the sale of liquor), the Dyer Act (prohibiting interstate transportation of stolen vehicles), and the Mann Act (an attempt on the federal level to curb prostitution). Largely because of those laws, the United States penitentiaries at Atlanta, Leavenworth, and McNeil Island became desperately crowded after World War I. As many as 4,000 men each were shoehorned into Atlanta and Leavenworth, institutions built for half as many. Because there was a lack of productive work for those inmates to do, and no inmate rehabilitation programs to speak of, most inmates were idle for most of the day—a potentially explosive situation.

Moreover, funding for those institutions was cut drastically, and administration was haphazard and inconsistent. The Superintendent of Prisons, a Justice Department official in Washington, was nominally in charge of the federal prisons. In reality, however, the superintendent exerted very little authority. Wardens at the individual prisons were political appointees who acted with considerable independence. The crowding and lack of central direction inhibited federal prisons in the 1920s from responding effectively to the advances in corrections philosophy that stressed the classification and individualized treatment of offenders.

Mabel Walker Willebrandt, the gifted Assistant Attorney General to whom the Superintendent of Prisons reported, instituted several important reforms in the 1920s. She established the reformatory for women in Alderson, West Virginia, and another for youthful offenders in Chillicothe, Ohio, and tried to expand work opportunities for prisoners. More was needed, however. This included a Federal Bureau of Prisons that would ensure consistent, centralized administration of federal prisons, professionalize the prison service, and provide more progressive and humane care for inmates.

The crowding and lack of central direction inhibited federal prisons in the 1920s from responding effectively to the advances in corrections philosophy.

Federal Bureau of Prisons

Sanford Bates, the well-respected Commissioner of Corrections in Massachusetts in the 1920s, became the first Director of the Federal Bureau of Prisons in 1930.

Director James Bennett (first row, fifth from left) held wardens' conferences annually to share ideas and ensure consistent administration throughout the growing federal prison system. Notable figures at the 1938 wardens' conference in Springfield, Missouri, include Alderson Warden Mary B. Harris (second row, second from left), Alcatraz Warden James Johnston (first row, third from right), and future Bureau of Prisons Director Myrl Alexander (top row, far right).

Inspired by a report written by future Federal Bureau of Prisons Director James V. Bennett, endorsed by a special committee of the United States House of Representatives, and pushed strongly by Willebrandt, legislation establishing the Bureau and mandating other prison reforms was enacted on May 14, 1930. Sanford Bates (1884-1972), former commissioner of corrections in Massachusetts and one of the leading prison reformers of his day, was named the first director of the Federal Bureau of Prisons.

Under Bates and his successor, Bennett, the Bureau created a highly diversified prison system by building or acquiring new institutions, ranging from minimum-security camps to the maximum-security penitentiary at Alcatraz, to a large hospital for federal prisoners at Springfield, Missouri. That expansion relieved crowding and, coupled with administrative reforms, enabled the Bureau to house inmates at the most appropriate security level and to offer inmates more opportunities for meaningful work and vastly improved educational and vocational training programs. In addition, the Federal Bureau of Prisons established an innovative training school for officers and placed Bureau staff under the authority of the Civil Service System, to root out political influence and cronyism.

Federal Bureau of Prisons

Sanford Bates and James Bennett brought in some of the most creative thinkers in corrections, including Austin MacCormick from New York and F. Lovell Bixby from New Jersey. The programs and facilities they designed had great influence over other prison systems in the country. The Federal Bureau of Prisons exercised even more direct influence through its jail inspection service, which demanded improvements in county jails and other facilities that held federal prisoners on a contract basis.

Bates' first major project as the Bureau's Director was the establishment of the Northeastern Penitentiary in Lewisburg, Pennsylvania, in 1932. Lewisburg Penitentiary vividly demonstrated the new directions of Bates' reign. It represented important changes in design, programs, and operations that would be a blueprint for the Bureau's future.

Lewisburg's design, by preeminent prison architect Alfred Hopkins (1870-1941), was a radical departure for American prisons. Instead of an oppressive, dismal, Bastille-like structure, Lewisburg was executed in an exquisite Italian Renaissance style, using cast stone, concrete blocks, and rough kiln bricks that gave it the appearance of a monastery or university. The "pleasing" architecture, Bates hoped, would enhance the rehabilitation program.

Staff training was fundamental to enhance the professionalism of correctional officers. Warden William Hiatt addresses a training class at the United States Penitentiary at Lewisburg in the early 1940s.

Federal Bureau of Prisons

Federal Bureau of Prisons

Alfred Hopkins (1870-1941), architect of the United States Penitentiary at Lewisburg.

The architecture had other benefits. Departing from the traditional, Auburn-style, flanking cellblocks with inside cells that was the most common prison design in the United States, Lewisburg was set out in the "telephone pole" style pioneered by prisons in France and at Wormwood Scrubs Prison in England: a central corridor bisected parallel cellhouses that ran at right angles off the corridor. The design was considered to enhance security. At the same time, Lewisburg was designed with diversified housing that would improve inmate classification. Rather than uniform steel cell housing, there were various types of housing: a few steel cells for the most desperate and intractable; about 400 securely guarded rooms with outside windows for the less dangerous; and 1,000 spaces in relatively open dormitories and single occupancy honor rooms for those requiring the least security.

Federal Bureau of Prisons

The United States Penitentiary at Lewisburg was designed to be more humane and even uplifting, and to look less like a prison.

A classification committee was formed at Lewisburg, the first ever in a federal prison for men. There was ample work for inmates in a metal furniture factory, and education courses were conducted in spacious classrooms. The modern, well-equipped infirmary was staffed by officers from the United States Public Health Service. Because it was the Bureau's most advanced men's prison at that time, the officers' training school was moved there (although it would soon be closed due to budget cuts). As Bates wished, Lewisburg was designed and administered in harmony with the objectives of scientific penology, and, as such, it was a microcosm of the Bureau's early endeavors.

Commissioned officers of the United States Public Health Service—physicians, psychiatrists, pharmacists, dentists, and nurses—provided medical care at the United States Medical Center for Federal Prisoners (below), which opened in Springfield, Missouri, in 1933.

Federal Bureau of Prisons

Federal Bureau of Prisons

Reform and Retribution: An Illustrated History of American Prisons

Federal Bureau of Prisons

The Federal Correctional Institution at Sandstone, Minnesota, built in 1939, arranged offices, classrooms, and housing units in long buildings that formed a large square, enclosing the prison yard. The four-sided design was used frequently by prisons built in the 1930s and 1940s. In this recent photograph, factory and warehouse buildings lie outside the main facility (above and to the left); the satellite camp on the right was added in the 1980s.

The front of the Federal Correctional Institution at LaTuna, Texas (built in 1934) was designed to fit in with its El Paso surroundings. Behind the administration building, the cellhouse design was similar to that of the Federal Correctional Institution at Sandstone.

Federal Bureau of Prisons

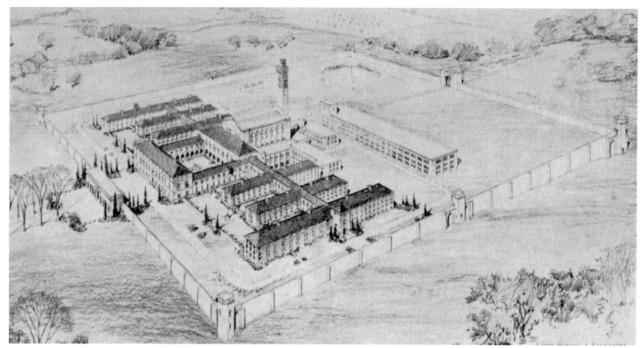

Federal Bureau of Prisons

Federal Bureau of Prisons

Architectural drawing and photograph of the United States Penitentiary at Lewisburg show telephone pole design of housing units, with classrooms and administrative offices front and center, a factory in the rear, and considerable space for recreation and farming.

Federal Bureau of Prisons

Federal Bureau of Prisons

Education and vocational training: arithmetic class, Women's Reformatory at Alderson, early 1940s; inmate library at the United States Penitentiary at Lewisburg, 1935; class in lettering and layout, the United States Penitentiary at Atlanta, 1939.

Federal Bureau of Prisons

Layout of modified telephone pole design at the United States Penitentiary at Terre Haute, Indiana.

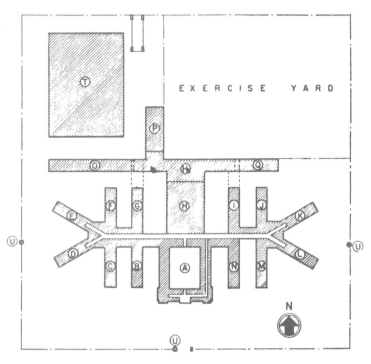

U.S. PENITENTIARY
TERRE HAUTE, INDIANA

A	ADMINISTRATION	H₁	KITCHEN	P	STORAGE
B	DORMITORY	I	MAXIMUM SECURITY	Q	LAUNDRY
C	HONOR ROOMS	J	CELL BLOCK (OUTSIDE)	R	POWER PLANT
D	CELL BLOCK (OUTSIDE)	K	" " "	S	GARAGE
E	" " "	L	" " "	T	INDUSTRIES
F	" " "	M	QUARANTINE	U	GUARD TOWERS
G	CONFINEMENT	N	HOSPITAL		
H	DINING, AUDITORIUM	O	MAINTENANCE SHOPS		

Federal Bureau of Prisons, *Handbook of Correctional Institution Design and Construction* (1949)

The prison at Fresnes, France, 1898, was one of the inspirations for the telephone pole design at the United States Penitentiary at Lewisburg.

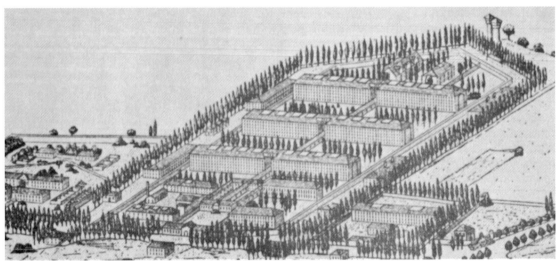

Federal Bureau of Prisons, *Handbook of Correctional Institution Design and Construction* (1949)

Reform and Retribution: An Illustrated History of American Prisons

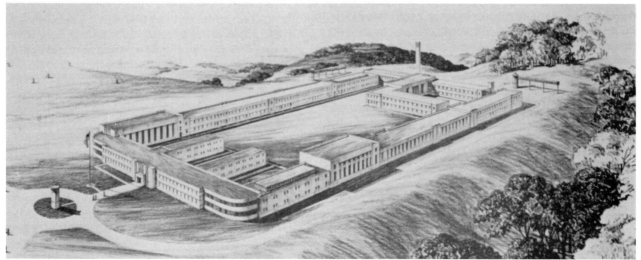

Federal Bureau of Prisons, *Handbook of Correctional Institution Design and Construction* (1949)

Architect's drawing of the Federal Correctional Institution at Danbury, Connecticut, a medium-security facility that opened in 1940.

Layout of the Danbury Federal Correctional Institution, which featured a self-enclosed or "open-box" design, like the Federal Correctional Institution at Sandstone, Minnesota.

FEDERAL CORRECTIONAL INSTITUTION
DANBURY, CONN.

100   0   100   200   300

N

A	ADMINISTRATION	I	LAUNDRY	Q	AUDITORIUM & SCHOOL
B	OUTSIDE CELL BLOCK	J	POWER HOUSE	R	OUTSIDE CELL BLOCK ◄
C	" " "	K	SHOP	S	GARAGE
D	INSIDE CELL BLOCK	L	"	T	GREENHOUSE
E	DORMITORY	M	WAREHOUSE	U	GUARD TOWERS
F	"	N	SHOP		
G	CUBICLE DORMITORY	O	KITCHEN		
H	HONOR ROOMS	P	DINING HALL	◄	ADMISSION UNIT

Federal Bureau of Prisons, *Handbook of Correctional Institution Design and Construction* (1949)

Another one of the Federal Bureau of Prisons' first undertakings which had a great impact on corrections was the creation of Federal Prison Industries, the most ambitious attempt yet to implement the state-use system. Not only did it propose to keep inmates at work, but it also sought to provide rehabilitative programming and to reach workable, meaningful compromises with organized labor and business interests that historically had opposed inmate labor schemes.

Under a law passed in 1934, Federal Prison Industries went into business on January 1, 1935, as a wholly owned government corporation that would employ inmates to produce a wide variety of merchandise in factories located in federal prisons. Federal Prison Industries operations would be labor-intensive to keep as many inmates as busy as possible. As a corporation, it would be completely self-supporting, operating on sales revenues rather than tax dollars. It would plow profits into inmate education, vocational training, and recreational programs, thereby helping fulfill its mission to rehabilitate inmates. Its revenues also would be used to pay stipends to inmates employed in its factories, as well as to inmates employed in other prison jobs.

Federal Prison Industries factory at the Federal Correctional Institution at El Reno, Oklahoma (built in the late 1930s).

Federal Bureau of Prisons, *Handbook of Correctional Institution Design and Construction* (1949)

Reform and Retribution: An Illustrated History of American Prisons

Federal Bureau of Prisons

The factory of the United States Penitentiary at Leavenworth which produced shoes, brooms, and brushes underwent expansion in the late 1930s.

Federal Bureau of Prisons

Chair factory under construction at the United States Reformatory in Chillicothe, Ohio (early 1930s).

To avoid engaging in unfair competition against the private sector, Federal Prison Industries would sell its products exclusively to agencies of the federal government. Moreover, it would diversify its product lines, so that it would not have an undue impact on any particular industry. By producing wooden furniture, metal furniture, shoes, brushes, blankets, printed materials, tents, gloves, apparel, grates, road signs, textiles, and other goods, and by limiting sales to the federal marketplace, Federal Prison Industries' overall market share in any one area would be insignificant. As an additional safeguard, business and organized labor were both represented on its Board of Directors, which had full authority over adopting, expanding, or deleting product lines.

Jobs for inmates in Federal Prison Industries' factories, plus jobs on the Federal Bureau of Prisons' farms, institutional assignments in food service, clerical and janitorial activities, and public works details (such as maintenance tasks on military bases and the building of federal roads) alleviated the scourge of idleness in federal prisons. Federal Prison Industries—which later adopted the trade name "Unicor"—was an unqualified success, and became the model for industrial enterprises in state prison systems.

Providing clerical support to prison administrators helped keep inmates constructively occupied (United States Penitentiary at Atlanta, late 1940s).

Federal Bureau of Prisons

Federal inmates manufacture signs for the National Park Service, 1940s.

Federal Bureau of Prisons

Federal Bureau of Prisons

The metal factory at the United States Penitentiary at Lewisburg in the late 1930s was one of the few federal prisons that ever manufactured license plates.

The Goal of Individualized Treatment   139

Juvenile Offenders

As corrections, in general, became increasingly influenced by the social sciences, services for juvenile offenders, in particular, received a boost from those disciplines during the early and mid-twentieth century. Inspired partly by the studies and recommendations of child psychologists, youth programs became highly rehabilitation-oriented. Eventually, they influenced adult corrections and anticipated the "Medical Model" programs of the 1960s.

Special courts and places of confinement for juveniles were not new. New York City and Boston opened houses of refuge for wayward, orphaned, or delinquent children in 1824 and 1825, respectively, and such facilities quickly proliferated—many of them being established by charitable and religious groups. State-run reform schools began appearing in the 1840s. The houses of refuge tended to emphasize rigid discipline and usually prevented residents from maintaining family ties. Reform schools, meanwhile, often were little more than sweatshops for exploiting child labor. Nonetheless, the children in houses of refuge and reform schools were safer and better cared for than they would have been in adult prisons, and sincere if meager efforts were made to educate and rehabilitate them.

Federal Bureau of Prisons, *Handbook of Correctional Institution Design and Construction* (1949)

The Philadelphia House of Refuge was established for juvenile offenders in 1860.

Maine Department of Corrections

State School for Boys, South Portland, Maine, 1939.

Federal Bureau of Prisons

Recent photograph of Federal Correctional Institution, El Reno, Oklahoma. The facility was built in 1934 to house younger offenders. It offered industrial and agricultural work and training opportunities.

The first court system for juveniles in the United States was established in Chicago by the State of Illinois in 1899. Juvenile courts had first appeared in England earlier in the century and were intended to protect the welfare of children by diverting them from the criminal courts, exercising considerable flexibility in sentencing, encouraging treatment over punishment when possible, and shielding young defendants from public scrutiny. It was not until 1925, however, that juvenile courts were in operation throughout the United States.

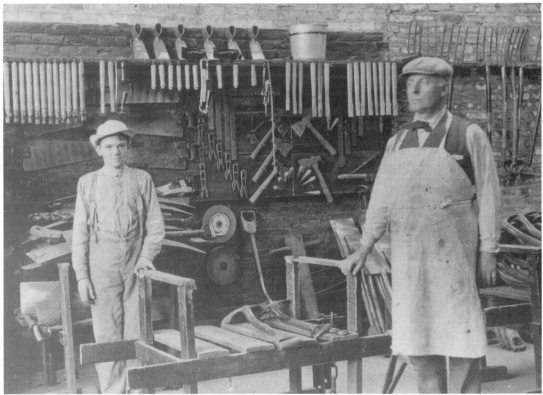

Indiana Department of Corrections

One of the earliest reformatories, the Indiana Youth Reformatory in the opening years of the twentieth century stressed vocational training and academic education classes (this page and opposite page).

Indiana Department of Corrections

Indiana Department of Corrections

Indiana Department of Corrections

The Goal of Individualized Treatment

Three years earlier, in 1922, Virginia became the first state to establish a separate corrections system for juveniles. Juvenile corrections systems or youth authorities sprang up in many states over the next twenty years. Typically, they enjoyed wide latitude in designating children to go to group homes, foster homes, or secure facilities, and most juveniles were committed under indeterminate sentences. The youth authorities were empowered to release the juvenile offenders whenever they considered them to be rehabilitated—or, they could keep them incarcerated until they were twenty-one years old.

The New Jersey State Youth Reformatory at Annandale featured separate cottages and an open campus layout.

Federal Bureau of Prisons, *Handbook of Correctional Institution Design and Construction* (1949)

Library at Indiana Youth Center, late 1970s.

Indiana Department of Corrections

Reform and Retribution: An Illustrated History of American Prisons

Federal Bureau of Prisons, *Handbook of Correctional Institution Design and Construction* (1949)

In the 1940s and 1950s, the Federal Prison Camp at Mill Point, West Virginia, put juvenile offenders to work on forestry projects.

The most ambitious and influential youth authority was the California Youth Authority, which was established in 1941. The federal government also established separate legal tracks for juveniles in 1938 with passage of the Federal Juvenile Delinquency Act. That law permitted United States Attorneys to prosecute youthful offenders for delinquency, rather than charging them with a specific crime; doing so permitted a wider range of treatment options, including probation. For those delinquents actually sentenced to a term of incarceration, the Federal Bureau of Prisons established or acquired several youth facilities. In 1950, at the strong urging of the Bureau of Prisons Director, James Bennett, Congress passed a more comprehensive law, the Youth Corrections Act, that authorized indeterminate sentences for federal juvenile offenders and mandated intensified treatment programs. By the 1950s and 1960s, the designation options, diagnostic services, and treatment programs that were first applied to juvenile offenders were being extended to adult offenders, as well.

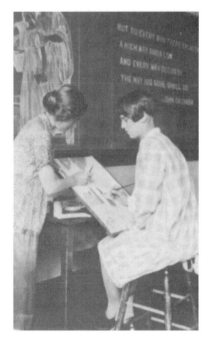

Reform and Retribution: An Illustrated History of American Prisons

Classroom study, basket-weaving, vocational training, vegetable harvesting, and recreational activities, at the Industrial School for Girls in Lancaster, Massachusetts, 1926.

Massachusetts Department of Corrections

Photo montage of the Federal Industrial Reformatory in Chillicothe, Ohio (ca. 1935) depicts industrial operations, education, vocational training, farming, basketball, track, and other activities for the youthful inmates.

Federal Bureau of Prisons

Reform and Retribution: An Illustrated History of American Prisons

Prisons in Wartime

An unprecedented feature of the American war effort after the United States entered World War II in 1941 was the extent to which state and federal inmates were avid and volunteer participants. Inmates contributed to the war effort in many ways: they gave blood, they purchased war bonds, and they even prepared to enter military service. A change in the law permitted ex-felons to enter the military, and tens of thousands of inmates were paroled directly from prison into the Army and Navy during World War II. Every federal prison apart from the maximum-security penitentiary at Alcatraz and the women's reformatory at Alderson had its own draft board to facilitate that process.

Without question, however, the greatest contribution of prisons was in the production of war material. Federal Prison Industries and similar industrial enterprises in state prison systems became important suppliers to the military. With its factories running at least two shifts per day, and some operating around the clock, Federal Prison Industries increased its production three fold between 1941 and 1945 and delivered $75 million of goods that went directly to the war effort. State prison production, meanwhile, exceeded $20 million of goods, with Michigan, Tennessee, and Ohio leading the way.

Chalk drawing of Adolph Hitler looms over inmates at the United States Penitentiary at Atlanta, early 1940s, reminding them of the importance of efficient wartime production.

Federal Bureau of Prisons

Prison factories manufactured tents, parachutes, cargo nets, ropes, mattresses, blankets, uniforms, even bomb fins and TNT cases. The Federal Prison Industries' shipyard at the McNeil Island Penitentiary built, remodeled, and repaired patrol boats, tugboats, and barges; the Tennessee State Prison constructed thirty pontoons a day for the Navy, and California's San Quentin Penitentiary built assault boats.

Inmates at Jackson State Prison, Michigan, construct assault boats for the U. S. Army.

Michigan Department of Corrections

Producing mattresses for the U. S. Army at Atlanta Penitentiary.

Federal Bureau of Prisons

Vocational training also was improved greatly in state and federal prisons to help the war effort. Courses in welding, blueprint reading, shipbuilding crafts, aviation mechanics, sheetmetal working, drafting, and other trades not only helped inmates in prison factories produce better products, but also prepared them to move directly from prison into jobs in defense factories. Particularly notable was the airplane mechanics school at the federal youth reformatory in Chillicothe, Ohio, which provided full-time training to inmates who could expect immediate placement following their release from prison in the all-important aircraft industry.

Federal Bureau of Prisons Director James Bennett (left) and Warden Joseph Sanford (right) escort United States Attorney General Francis Biddle on a tour of the United States Penitentiary at Atlanta in January 1942, during which Biddle inspected factories producing war materials for the U.S. Armed Forces.

Federal Bureau of Prisons

Army patrol boat under construction at the United States Penitentiary at McNeil Island shipyard.

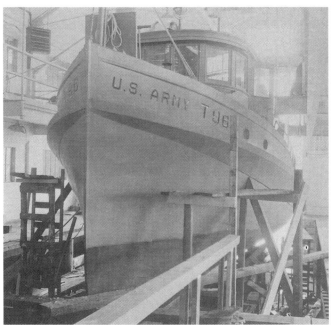

Federal Bureau of Prisons

American Correctional Association

Inmates build model airplanes for use in training military pilots to identify friendly and enemy aircraft.

Food production on prison farms also soared. That eased burdens on the nation's food supply by making prisons practically self-sufficient. In addition, some of the food from prison farms was processed in prison canneries for shipment to the military.

The high levels of production were achieved despite the fact that the prison population declined during the war—mainly because so many men between eighteen and forty years of age were in the military.

The war, however, did bring an influx of selective service violators into federal prison, along with conscientious objectors who refused to participate in the war effort. Federal Bureau of Prisons Director Bennett admonished his wardens to exercise "utmost tact and patience . . . when considering their political or religious views," and stated that they were not "criminal in the generally accepted sense of the term." Indeed, they were not. More literate and politically sophisticated than the average prisoner before the war, and often from law-abiding, middle class or upper class backgrounds, those inmates presented unusual challenges to prison administrators. Ultimately, they demanded—and often won—significant changes in the prison environment. Among the reforms they precipitated were greater access to outside publications, less censorship of prisoner correspondence, and the first glimmerings of racial desegregation behind bars.

Inmates at Rhode Island Reformatory do their part for the wartime blood drive, 1943.

Rhode Island Department of Corrections

Federal Bureau of Prisons

Military uniforms are manufactured at Jackson State Prison in Michigan.

Production of steel bars at Rhode Island State Reformatory.

Rhode Island Department of Corrections

First Lady Eleanor Roosevelt, accompanied by former U.S. Representative and head of defense production Maury Maverick (holding overcoat), visiting factory at the Maryland Penitentiary in Baltimore, which produced furniture for the U.S. Armed Forces (1943).

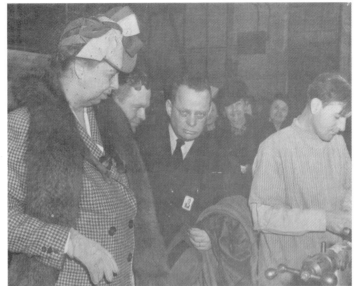

Maryland Department of Corrections

Textile production, Attica State Prison, New York.

New York Department of Corrections

Reform and Retribution: An Illustrated History of American Prisons

California Department of Corrections

The auditorium at San Quentin Penitentiary, California, was used for assembling ration books for civilian distribution, 1943.

Poster exhorts inmates of the United States Penitentiary at Atlanta to contribute to the war effort.

Federal Bureau of Prisons

Reform and Retribution: An Illustrated History of American Prisons

Alcatraz

Federal Bureau of Prisons Director Sanford Bates did not want Alcatraz. His successor, James V. Bennett, tried to get rid of it as early as 1939. It was the most famous of all federal prisons, dramatically perched on a rock in the middle of San Francisco Bay: the United States Penitentiary at Alcatraz. Originally a military prison, it was acquired by the Justice Department in 1933, retrofitted, and reopened for business as the Federal Bureau of Prisons' most secure facility in 1934.

Floor plan of the United States Penitentiary at Alcatraz.

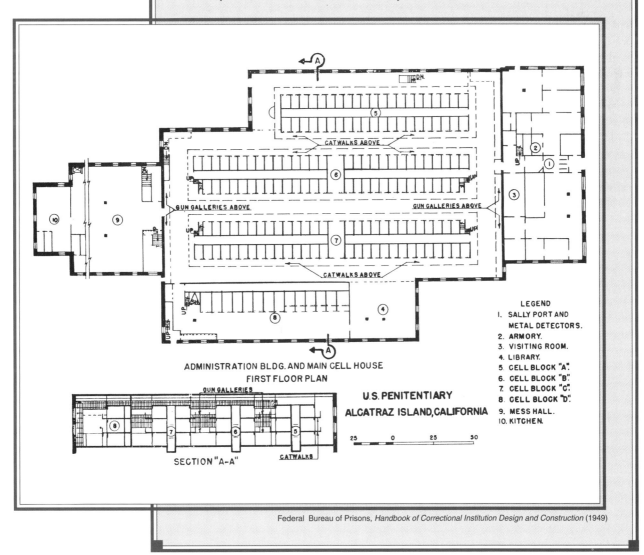

ADMINISTRATION BLDG. AND MAIN CELL HOUSE
FIRST FLOOR PLAN

SECTION "A-A"

U.S. PENITENTIARY
ALCATRAZ ISLAND, CALIFORNIA

25   0   25   50

LEGEND
1. SALLY PORT AND METAL DETECTORS.
2. ARMORY.
3. VISITING ROOM.
4. LIBRARY.
5. CELL BLOCK "A".
6. CELL BLOCK "B".
7. CELL BLOCK "C".
8. CELL BLOCK "D".
9. MESS HALL.
10. KITCHEN.

Federal Bureau of Prisons, *Handbook of Correctional Institution Design and Construction* (1949)

Federal Bureau of Prisons

The United States Penitentiary at Alcatraz (above) helped make rehabilitation programs possible by segregating the most violent inmates so that they could not disrupt other prisons. The cellhouse is at the top of the hill; staff housing, dock facilities, the power plant, the factory, and other support buildings cling to the perimeter of the rocky island.

Part of the Alcatraz staff on opening day, 1934. Officer Royal Cline (standing, third from left) was bludgeoned to death five years later by three would-be escapees.

Federal Bureau of Prisons

Intended as the Justice Department's answer to the gangsters who plagued the country in the 1930s, Alcatraz housed some of America's most notorious criminals: Al Capone, Machine Gun Kelly, and Alvin "Creepy" Karpis, among others. The "Birdman," Robert Stroud, was also there. He did not have his birds at Alcatraz, though, and, far from being the sort of kindly gentleman portrayed by Burt Lancaster in the popular movie, was a homicidal sociopath who loved birds, according to one Attorney General, but hated people.

Alcatraz was a maximum-security, minimum-privilege prison that housed the Federal Bureau of Prisons' toughest cases. To Bates and Bennett, it seemed like a throwback to the pure punishment model of corrections, and also seemed to contradict their emphasis on individualized treatment and rehabilitation.

In reality, both Bates and Bennett were able to use Alcatraz to further their goals of individual treatment and more humane confinement. By sending the worst desperados to the Rock, they were able to loosen some of the restrictions at other prisons and offer more programs to inmates—programs that Alcatraz-bound inmates would have disrupted had they been given the chance.

"Broadway," the central corridor in the Alcatraz cellhouse.

Federal Bureau of Prisons

Myths about Alcatraz abound, spread by a few former inmates and seized upon by film makers and pulp fiction writers. But the myths have little historical validity. When it was open, Alcatraz was visited by members of Congress, judges, and members of civic organizations, none of whom found anything amiss. Alcatraz was an extremely sanitary prison and a very tightly run operation that was closely supervised by Washington.

Alcatraz was always an expensive prison to run, partly because it cost so much to transport prisoners all the way out to the West Coast, partly because all of its supplies, including water and fuel, had to be barged out to the island, and partly because it was so old that it needed several million dollars' worth of renovations. When public attitudes shifted briefly in favor of rehabilitation in the 1960s, the Federal Bureau of Prisons was able to abandon Alcatraz. However, it had proven so conclusively the value of concentrating the worst and most dangerous offenders that even James Bennett, who had campaigned to close it down for many years, recognized the need to replace it with a new maximum-security prison: the United States Penitentiary at Marion, Illinois.

Alcatraz inmates walk down steps from the recreation yard to their work assignments in the laundry, which did cleaning not only for the prison but also for military bases up and down the West Coast (ca. 1945).

Federal Bureau of Prisons

Federal Bureau of Prisons

In the 1940s, dominoes and handball were popular diversions for inmates in the small recreation yard adjacent to the Alcatraz cellhouse.

Federal Bureau of Prisons

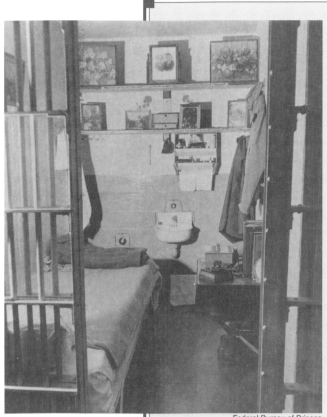

Captain Philip Bergen in the 15,000 volume inmate library, ca. 1950.

Federal Bureau of Prisons

Federal Bureau of Prisons

To maintain discipline and protect the inmates from each other, Alcatraz never deviated from a "one man-one cell" policy.

"D Block" served as the disciplinary segregation unit for the United States Penitentiary at Alcatraz.

Federal Bureau of Prisons

Robert Stroud, the notorious "Birdman of Alcatraz." First incarcerated for murder in 1909, he beat a fellow inmate nearly to death a few years later at the United States Penitentiary at McNeil Island and murdered an officer at Leavenworth in 1915. Permitted to keep and study birds in his double cell at Leavenworth, his bird cages, feed, and scientific equipment hid various weapons and a fully operational still. Denied an aviary after he was transferred to Alcatraz, Stroud continued to write about birds—but he was not the placid, gentlemanly scientist portrayed in the movies. Alcatraz Captain Philip Bergen recalled that "Stroud was a Jekyll and Hyde character—and you never knew when he got up in the morning which one he would be."

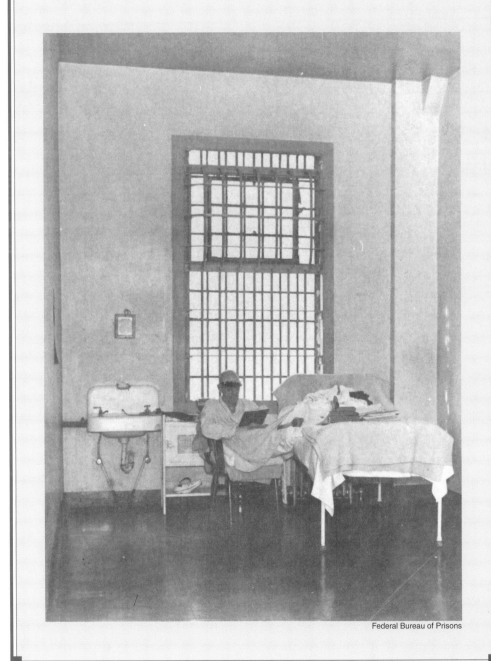

Federal Bureau of Prisons

Postwar Tensions and the Medical Model

7

Texas Department of Corrections

Inmates peer through bars at a state prison in Texas.

Ever since the appearance of the penitentiary in the late eighteenth century, the concept of reform or rehabilitation as an element in the prison experience has been debated, refined, and expanded. It always had been a goal, but the emphasis it was given and the means employed to achieve it changed dramatically. The Pennsylvania System would induce reform through solitary Bible-readings, meditation, and hard work; the Elmira System, endorsed—but did not always provide—classification, education, and incentives for good behavior as an alternative to sanctions for misbehavior. By the 1920s and 1930s, the Elmira System was being rehabilitated, with more sophisticated programs and classification methods, innovative designs, and an intellectual grounding in the social sciences.

The rehabilitation ideal reached its zenith in the 1960s with the so-called "Medical Model." The Medical Model invested the most hope and confidence in the rehabilitation ideal ever, and proposed some of the most radical departures in prison operations. It did not come into prominence, however, until after a rash of disturbances hit the country's prisons in the post-World War II era, and helped focus public attention on prison deficiencies and the need for new approaches.

To avoid the buildup of tension at Texas state prisons, as well as to prepare inmates for reentry into society, programs including classes in automobile mechanics were developed.

Texas Department of Corrections

A Period of Unrest

On May 2, 1946, six inmates at the U.S. Penitentiary at Alcatraz took nine officers hostage, captured firearms, and held a cellblock for two days before prison staff aided by the U.S. Marines were able to regain control. Two officers died and three inmates were killed in what became known as the "Alcatraz Blastout."

The Alcatraz Blastout was the first in a series of riots that rocked prisons and grabbed headlines after World War II. Although the Alcatraz Blastout was little more than an escape attempt on the part of a few inmates that went awry, many of the other riots stemmed from deeper grievances over systemic problems in prison operations, and involved large numbers of inmates.

Scores of riots flared up in the 1950s. March through June of 1952 were especially violent months, with destructive riots at state prisons in Trenton, New Jersey; Bordentown, New Jersey; Rahway, New Jersey; Jackson, Michigan; Concord, Massachusetts; Soledad, California; and elsewhere. Later in 1952, riots broke out at the Ohio State Penitentiary in Columbus; Menard State Prison in Illinois; the state penitentiaries in Utah and New Mexico; and at federal youth reformatories in El Reno, Oklahoma, and Chillicothe, Ohio.

(Below and opposite) Armed correctional officers and policemen bring a riot at Jackson State Prison in Michigan under control. The Jackson State riot was one of a series of prison disturbances that flared up across the United States in 1952.

Michigan Department of Corrections

Reform and Retribution: An Illustrated History of American Prisons

The violence continued into 1953, with major disturbances at New Mexico State Penitentiary, Western State Penitentiary near Pittsburgh, and at another Pennsylvania state prison in Rockview. The state prison in Jefferson City, Missouri, erupted the following year, and in 1955 there was an uprising at the state prison in Charlestown, Massachusetts. Numerous other riots also occurred during that period.

Michigan Department of Corrections

Michigan Department of Corrections

Debris litters prison yard following riot at Jackson State Prison.

The disturbances were the result of dislocations that appeared in American prison systems after World War II. When the war ended, the decline in the prison population was reversed; soon, the prison population surpassed pre-war levels, and crowding—especially in state prisons—was becoming acute. Further, the end of the war suddenly eliminated most of the demand for prison-made goods. Federal Prison Industries was able to mitigate the effects of lost defense orders by turning to the backlog of orders from federal civilian agencies that had built up during the war, developing new product lines, and employing inmates in the lucrative field of repairing or reconditioning government-owned furniture and business machines. State prisons were not as fortunate, and idleness became a serious concern as state prison factories had fewer and fewer orders to fill.

Federal Prison Industries' Board of Directors commented on the situation in 1954, observing that "The prison riots and disturbances which have occurred so extensively in state prisons throughout the country in the past two years have demonstrated most effectively and at a tragic cost the absolute necessity for a well-planned and comprehensive work and production program.... (L)arge groups of idle prisoners create a constant hazardous situation. The deteriorating effect of long periods of idleness in prison is in turn one of the major causes of the unrest and tensions underlying the costly and destructive outbreaks."

Attorney General Tom Clark (far right), in front of Alcatraz cellhouse, speaks at a memorial service for officers slain in the 1946 Alcatraz "Blastout."

Federal Bureau of Prisons

Reform and Retribution: An Illustrated History of American Prisons

American Correctional Association

American Correctional Association

American Prison Association presidents, Richard A. McGee installed in 1943 (top) and James V. Bennett installed in 1940 (bottom).

Federal Bureau of Prisons Director James V. Bennett (far left) and U.S. Attorney General Tom Clark speak with inmates at the United States Penitentiary at Atlanta, in the late 1940s.

The American Prison Association (successor to the old National Prison Association) appointed a special committee to assess the riots. Chaired by California's widely respected Commissioner of Corrections, Richard A. McGee (1897-1983), the committee's report in 1953 confirmed that the chief causes of the riots were inmate idleness and gross crowding, as well as some prisons being so large that they could not be managed safely. The report also criticized the lack of funding for education and other treatment programs, poorly trained officers, excessive political interference in prison management, and public indifference to prison needs and objectives. The report also was critical of anti-crime crusades that led to longer sentences and delayed paroles—thereby increasing not only the number of inmates but also their desperation and hopelessness.

The American Prison Association and leading prison administrators—McGee in California, Russell Oswald in Wisconsin, and the Federal Bureau of Prisons' James Bennett, among others—responded to the crisis by reinforcing the treatment aspect of incarceration and trying to steer public policy and public opinion away from traditional notions of punishment. Part of the response was semantic: the American Prison Association changed its name to the American Correctional Association, for example, and the accepted term for a disciplinary segregation cell became "adjustment center," rather than "the hole." Yet, there was also a burst of energy in corrections lasting through the 1960s that made behavioral science-based rehabilitation programs and the establishment of more humane conditions the primary focus of corrections.

Federal Bureau of Prisons

The Medical Model

In its simplest terms, the Medical Model was a theory of corrections that viewed criminality as analogous to a physical disease. It was the role of prison to diagnose the causes of criminality in an individual—social immaturity, psychological maladjustment, alcohol or drug abuse, illiteracy, lack of job skills—and to prescribe a regimen to cure the illness. Treatment programs might involve behavior modification therapy, psychological counseling, addiction therapy, vocational training, or whatever would help induce rehabilitation.

In 1970, the Joint Commission on Correctional Manpower and Training succinctly stated the conception and policy implications of the Medical Model:

> "The offender is to be perceived as a person with social, intellectual, or emotional deficiencies who should be diagnosed carefully and his deficiencies clinically defined. Programs should be designed to correct these deficiencies to the point that would permit him to assume a productive, law-abiding place in the community. To achieve these goals of correctional treatment, it would be necessary only to maintain the pressure on the inmate for his participation in the treatment programs, to continue to humanize institutional living, to upgrade the educational level of the line officer, and to expand the complement of professional treatment and training personnel."

Diagnostic Center in Menlo Park, New Jersey, 1950.

New Jersey Department of Corrections

To make diagnoses, many state prison systems in the 1950s and 1960s established reception and diagnostic centers. Incoming prisoners would begin their sentences at those centers, undergoing medical and psychiatric examinations, sitting for clinical interviews to establish social, vocational, educational, and family histories, and taking batteries of psychological tests and aptitude examinations.

Inmates would be classified based on the diagnoses, and could be reclassified later as institutional adjustment and treatment program performance warranted. Highly sophisticated and elaborately structured classification systems were devised during the Medical Model era, such as Quay Typology. Named for its originator, Professor Herbert Quay of Temple University, Quay Typology divided offenders into five personality categories: inadequate-immature, neurotic-conflicted, unsocialized-aggressive, socialized or subcultural, and subcultural-immature.

The Reception and Guidance Center at Jackson State Prison, Michigan. New inmates were segregated from the general population during their first month in prison, as staff developed housing, work, and other program assignments for them.

Michigan Department of Corrections

In theory, treatment programs would be customized for the particular personality type or classification category. In addition to such traditional treatment options as prison-based work assignments, education courses, and vocational training programs, there were work release, study release, group counseling, and even special living units designed to deliver intensified treatment to drug addicts, sex offenders, or inmates presenting chronic disciplinary problems. Correctional officers received additional training to help them advance the treatment process, and prison systems recruited armies of teachers, counselors, case managers, and psychologists. Not all prison systems or individual facilities, however, had the resources or political support to implement such programs.

As part of the process for devising treatment programs, new inmates at the Elmira (New York) Reception Center (as shown in 1959) took batteries of intelligence and psychological tests and met with counselors.

Photo by M. Dixson, New York State Health Department

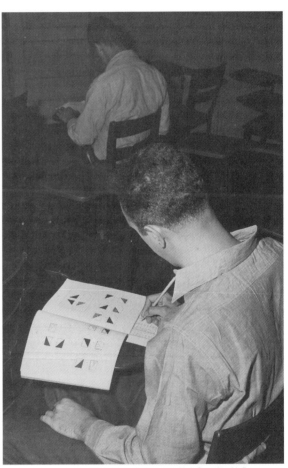

Photo by M. Dixson, New York State Health Department

Among some of the specialized programs in the Federal Bureau of Prisons, for example, were "Asklepieion," which used transactional analysis to promote self-help attitudes, "CASE," which offered incentives to youthful offenders to succeed at education programs, and drug abuse treatment units throughout the system, as provided for by the Narcotics Addicts Rehabilitation Act. Another was "START," or the Special Treatment and Rehabilitative Training unit established in 1972 at the Federal Bureau of Prisons' Medical Center in Springfield, Missouri. Residents of the unit were highly disruptive inmates who otherwise faced continuous lockdown because they were such a threat to officers and fellow inmates. START offered rewards to inmates who managed to keep their living areas clean, complete work assignments, and avoid such disruptive behavior as assaulting people. Inmate advocacy groups argued that START was punishment-based rather than therapeutic. Some attacked it as brainwashing and thought control—a ludicrous misreading of a very modest program—but it was enough to end START and send many of its participants back to continuous lockdown.

Federal Bureau of Prisons

Treatment programs included substance abuse initiatives (above) at an unidentified federal prison in 1970 and group therapy (right), Federal Correctional Institution, Seagoville, Texas, ca. 1950.

Federal Bureau of Prisons

Treatment programs included vocational training, education, and even wholesome recreational activities. Pictured: Linotype training at the Federal Correctional Institution, El Reno, Oklahoma, 1960; academic studies at a Texas state prison; band practice, United States Penitentiary at Alcatraz, 1950s; and an inmate library, in a Texas state prison (ca. 1968).

Texas Department of Corrections

Federal Bureau of Prisons

Federal Bureau of Prisons

Texas Department of Corrections

Functional unit management emerged during the Medical Model era because it was a better way of delivering treatment, and it remained in general use long after the Medical Model was abandoned because it was a highly efficient method of prison administration. Unit management divided the prison into semi-autonomous housing units or "mini prisons," each of which was under the supervision of a unit manager.

In some cases, units specialized in a particular type of treatment—handling offenders with histories of drug abuse, for example—but most units housed general population inmates. Factories, education classes, recreation areas, and mess halls usually were common areas, although units at some prisons were completely self-contained. Generally, however, only the living units were self-contained, with staff members permanently assigned to them. Having the same unit staff working day-to-day with the same group of inmates encouraged greater interaction between staff and inmates, permitted closer monitoring of inmate activities, better casework, and faster response to inmate concerns.

Modern unit management appeared in the late 1960s and early 1970s at such facilities as the Federal Correctional Institution in Morgantown, West Virginia, but some of the earliest harbingers were apparent in the cottage arrangement of the women's reformatory in Alderson, decades earlier. By the 1980s, functional unit management was in wide use throughout American corrections.

Industrial programs were an important component of the Medical Model. Federal Bureau of Prisons Director Myrl Alexander (light overcoat) visits the factory at the United States Penitentiary at Lewisburg with Attorney General Ramsey Clark standing next to Alexander, ca. 1968.

Federal Bureau of Prisons

Inmate leaving the Federal Reformatory at Alderson, ca 1965. Under the Medical Model, release planning received greater attention than ever before, as work-release programs and halfway houses were developed to help ease the offender's reentry into the community.

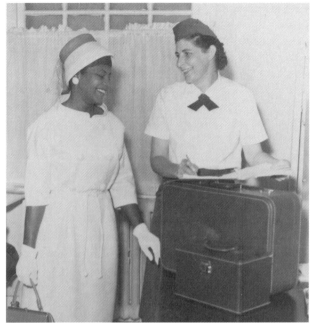

Federal Bureau of Prisons

Religious services have been central to American prison life since the eighteenth century. Pictured: services at an unidentified state prison, 1960s, and at the United States Penitentiary at Atlanta, 1940s. By the 1960s and 1970s, Islamic services and Native American worship were becoming increasingly common in American prisons, along with Catholic, Protestant, and Jewish services, which had long been available.

American Correctional Association

Federal Bureau of Prisons

Federal Bureau of Prisons

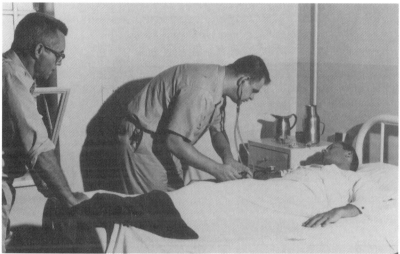

Federal Bureau of Prisons

In the 1950s, the U.S. Public Health Service continued to provide medical care for federal prisoners.

Efforts to make prison less repressive during the Medical Model era: (bottom left) inmates at the Federal Correctional Institution, LaTuna, Texas, listen to a radio during their nonworking hours, ca 1950; (bottom right) inmates at San Quentin Penitentiary, California, use headphones to hear radio programs approved by the warden, 1940s.

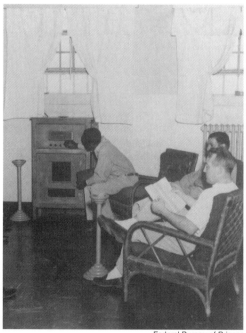

Federal Bureau of Prisons

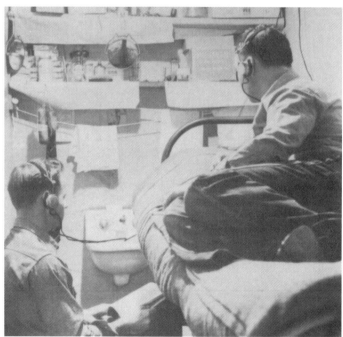

California Department of Corrections

Changes in prison architecture enhanced Medical Model treatment programs. Decentralized compounds made specialized treatment and unit management easier by replacing traditional cellblocks with separate cottages or units. More attractive designs theoretically made prisons more therapeutic and less demoralizing, and fit well with less-stringent control over inmate activities. The long tables and benches that formerly had prevailed in grim prison mess halls were replaced with more relaxed (and more efficient) cafeteria-style feeding. Multitiered, Auburn-style cellblocks gave way to modular housing units, with two levels of cells surrounding an open common area, which was more comfortable for the inmates, less expensive to build, and easier to supervise.

Warm weather allowed inmates to visit outdoors at the United States Penitentiary at Lewisburg, late 1950s.

Federal Bureau of Prisons

The commissary at the United States Penitentiary at Atlanta sold snacks and toiletries to inmates, late 1940s.

Federal Bureau of Prisons

The movement toward less regimented prisons continued a trend begun during the Reformatory Era to "normalize" the prison environment. Doing away with the silent system, the lockstep, and striped uniforms were early examples of the trend. By the 1920s and 1930s, commissaries in some prisons allowed inmates to use their modest prison earnings to purchase candy, snacks, toiletries, and tobacco, and by the 1940s and 1950s, many prisons installed earphone jacks into cells to permit inmates to listen to one or two radio stations selected by the wardens. Soon, more comfortable and informal visiting rooms were typical, and by the 1960s, there were televisions in common areas, less censorship of inmate mail, and greater access to newspapers and magazines. Such innovations helped reduce tension within prisons and were intended to encourage healthier community living that would help prepare inmates for their return to society.

Barracks living at Kulani Prison in Hawaii (note rows of bunks and lockers through doorway at left) is improved by a pleasant dayroom with a fireplace and television set.

Hawaii Department of Corrections (photo by R. Wenkam)

Barracks-like open dormitory in a federal prison, 1940s.

Federal Bureau of Prisons

Inmate dining evolved from mess halls with long, uncomfortable benches (Federal Correctional Institution, LaTuna, Texas, ca. 1950) to a more relaxed environment featuring cafeteria-style tables (Federal Correctional Institution, Petersburg, Virginia, 1960).

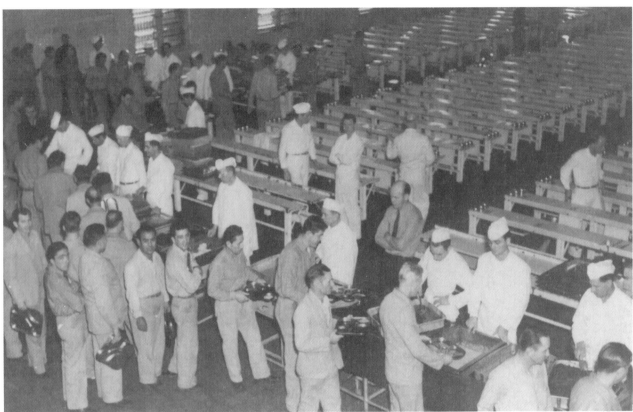

Federal Bureau of Prisons

Federal Bureau of Prisons

Reform and Retribution: An Illustrated History of American Prisons

Early prototypes for the new type of prison included state facilities in Wallkill, New York; Chino, California; and Norfolk, Massachusetts; as well as the Federal Correctional Institution in Seagoville, Texas. James Bennett was especially proud of the Seagoville facility, which he liked to call "the prison without walls."

Bennett said that Seagoville, with its strong programming emphasis, lack of regimentation, and pleasing design was "living proof that there may be no need to build costly cellblocks except for a few chronic escape artists, a few desperados, and a few who have lost all hope." Cinching Seagoville's "prison community" concept for the frugal Bennett was the fact that facilities in the Seagoville mold could be built for one-half or one-third the per-inmate cost of constructing a high-security penitentiary.

Arizona Department of Corrections

Inmate food line, Arizona State Penitentiary, Florence (1971).

Dining area, Leesburg, New Jersey, ca. 1975.

New Jersey Department of Corrections

Federal Bureau of Prisons

Federal Correctional Institution, Seagoville, Texas, was a principal site for the Federal Bureau of Prisons' Medical Model innovations in the 1940s and 1950s.

Federal Bureau of Prisons, *Handbook of Correctional Institution Design and Construction* (1949)

Aerial view of Seagoville's open campus design.

National Archives

Jazz great Louis Armstrong performs for inmates at the United States Penitentiary at Lewisburg, 1957.

Sources for Medical Model ideas included experimental prison programs being developed in Britain and Scandinavia. A more immediate source was juvenile corrections in the United States. Under the dynamic leadership of Commissioner of Corrections Richard McGee, the California prison system began adopting programs first implemented by California's Youth Corrections Authority. Similarly, throughout the 1950s and 1960s, James Bennett introduced programs from federal youth facilities into adult institutions. And Bennett was the guiding force behind the Prisoner Rehabilitation Act of 1965 (enacted the year after he retired), that extended to adult federal inmates the sort of diagnostic services and treatment programs previously accorded mainly to youthful offenders.

Federal Bureau of Prisons, *Handbook of Correctional Institution Design and Construction* (1949)

Acceptable and easily supervised recreational activities: inmates at the U.S. Penitentiary, Atlanta, play football and softball, late 1940s.

Massachusetts Department of Corrections

One of the first male institutions to move away from the more regimented, traditional prison structure was the State Prison Colony in Norfolk, Massachusetts (opened in 1931), which featured dormitory units instead of cellblocks.

Massachusetts Department of Corrections

Floor plan of New York State's innovative Wallkill Prison included ample space for reading, recreational activities, and work, and featured Eastern State Penitentiary-style "outside" rooms.

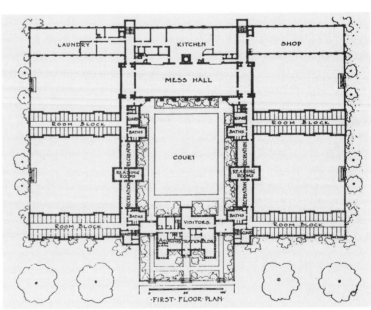

Federal Bureau of Prisons, *Handbook of Correctional Institution Design and Construction* (1949)

Reform and Retribution: An Illustrated History of American Prisons

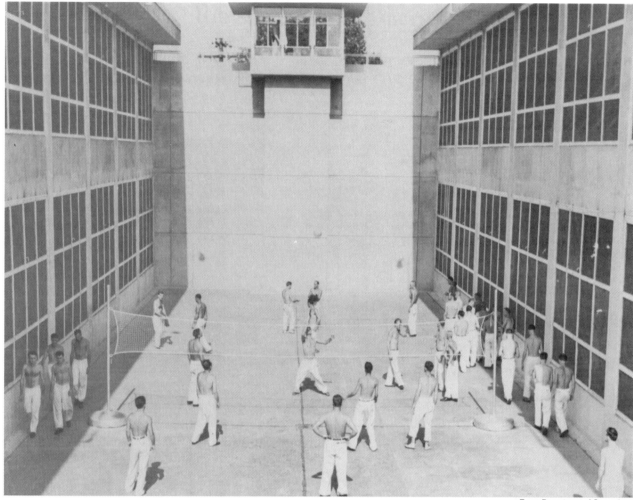

Texas Department of Corrections

(Above) Inside exercise yard of the segregation unit at Huntsville State Penitentiary, Texas. (Below, left) a control center at bottom of steps to a multi-tiered cellblock at a Texas state prison. (Below, right) Inmates move along a corridor from work assignments to mess hall at a federal prison, ca. 1948.

Texas Department of Corrections

Federal Bureau of Prisons, *Handbook of Correctional Institution Design and Construction* (1949)

American Correctional Association

George Beto, president of the American Correctional Association, 1966-1970.

Playing counterpoint to the Medical Model was the Control Model, developed in the Texas state prison system by Director George Beto (1916-1991), who took office in 1961. Beto had assisted his predecessor, O.B. Ellis, in drastically upgrading the appalling living conditions in Texas prisons in the 1950s. After he became Director, however, Beto took a course that advocated strict discipline. All elements of an inmate's daily routine were tightly regimented, and absolute and immediate compliance with officers' instructions was required. Obedient inmates received good time credits, but there was solitary confinement and added work awaiting those who were disobedient. The Control Model soon brought a torrent of lawsuits and helped usher in the judicial activism that played an unprecedented role in corrections by the 1970s and 1980s. Nonetheless, other state systems were influenced by the Control Model and adopted some of its elements.

California Medical Facility in Vacaville (opened in 1950).

Federal Bureau of Prisons

Reform and Retribution: An Illustrated History of American Prisons

New educational building at the Sumter County Correctional Institution in South Carolina nears completion, 1965.

South Carolina Department of Corrections

Texas Department of Corrections

The Wynne Unit of the Texas Department of Criminal Justice, Institutional Division, in Huntsville, Texas. The Wynne Unit was established in 1937 and covers approximately 1,433 acres. The inmate population includes first offenders and recidivists of all custodies.

Within the fence, the Vienna State Correctional Center in Illinois (opened in 1965) achieved a "normalized" environment, with small, decentralized housing units, and an open compound.

Illinois Department of Corrections

Reform and Retribution: An Illustrated History of American Prisons

Community Corrections

Community corrections became one of the Medical Model's most enduring legacies. Coming into general use in the 1960s, halfway houses, prerelease guidance centers, work and study release, and home confinement became essential components of the criminal justice system.

There were only a handful of halfway houses operating in the United States when U.S. Attorney General Robert F. Kennedy instructed the Federal Bureau of Prisons to develop a halfway house pilot program in 1961. Future Bureau Director Norman A. Carlson (1933-   ) took charge of the program, which established a series of "prerelease guidance centers" that would help youthful offenders make the transition from imprisonment to freedom.

Early halfway houses, such as this typical one, were operated by corrections agencies; many agencies, however, eventually began contracting for community corrections services with private sector and nonprofit organizations.

Federal Bureau of Prisons

The Bureau had operated prerelease units within prisons before, but these new centers were located in various types of buildings—an old monastery, a former YMCA—in urban neighborhoods. They were not secure facilities, although they closely monitored residents' activities. Residents were supervised from early evening until early morning, but they generally left the centers during the day to attend classes or go to work. The centers provided psychological counseling, job placement services, and instructions on all kinds of everyday living skills, from opening a bank account, to renting an apartment, to following proper table manners.

The prerelease guidance centers—later dubbed community treatment centers, community corrections centers, or halfway houses—helped inspire the Federal Prisoner Rehabilitation Act of 1965, which extended halfway house placement opportunities to adults. Dozens of state prison systems emulated the program.

Although many early halfway houses were owned and staffed by state or federal prison systems, by the 1980s many would be privately owned. The Federal Bureau of Prisons and state corrections agencies would place offenders in the privately owned facilities on a fee or contract basis.

Residents of the Detroit Prerelease Guidance Center enjoy coffee in the center's dining room.

Federal Bureau of Prisons

In some cases, nonviolent offenders with short sentences would serve their entire terms in halfway houses—thus freeing costlier bedspace in prisons for more serious offenders. More commonly, however, inmates would be assigned to halfway houses for only the last three to six months of their incarceration, so that they could have time to secure steady employment, establish positive ties to the community, and readjust from the institutional environment.

Another form of community corrections is home confinement. It is generally used as an alternative to jail detention for individuals awaiting trial, or—like halfway houses—as a transitional designation immediately prior to release. Like halfway house residents, individuals under home confinement usually are permitted to go to jobs during the day, but have to return home by an established curfew. Various means are employed to ensure that individuals under home confinement comply with the rules—such as locking electronic monitoring devices around their ankles or wrists.

Federal Bureau of Prisons

One of the first Federal Bureau of Prisons halfway houses, Los Angeles, (ca. 1962).

Co-corrections

In contrast to the success of community corrections, co-corrections—or the integration of male and female inmates—has had disappointing results.

Ironically, the integration of male and female inmates was one of the first problems attacked by prison reformers in the eighteenth century, and division by gender was the beginning of classification. Further, one of the avowed purposes of women's prisons was to rehabilitate women by separating them (and protecting them) from men. The Federal Correctional Institution at Terminal Island, California, housed both male and female prisoners as early as the 1950s, but, in reality, Terminal Island operated as two distinct facilities—one for men and one for women.

By the early 1970s, the option of integrating the sexes in co-correctional prisons seemed appropriate for several reasons. Proponents argued that co-corrections would create a less institutional, more normal social atmosphere for inmates than single-sex facilities, thereby preparing inmates for their return to the community. Co-correctional facilities also would give prison administrators more flexibility in designating inmates, relieving crowding, and permitting a more efficient use of prison space, staff, and program resources. Finally, co-corrections theoretically would give women greater access to programs and services, giving them parity with male inmates.

Co-correctional typing class, Federal Correctional Institution, Lexington, late 1970s.

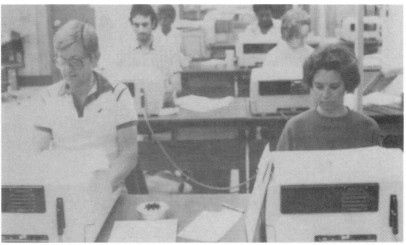

Federal Bureau of Prisons

In 1971, the Federal Bureau of Prisons designated its facilities at Fort Worth, Texas and Morgantown, West Virginia, as co-correctional prisons. Several other federal prisons went co-correctional in the ensuing years, including the Federal Correctional Institution in Lexington, Kentucky in 1974, as did nearly fifty state prisons in about two dozen states.

Started with the best of intentions, co-correctional facilities proved difficult to manage and did not live up to expectations. Research showed a tendency in co-correctional institutions for negative sex-role stereotypes to be reinforced in both male and female inmates. There was evidence that male inmates exploited female inmates. Most frustrating for prison administrators trying to equalize program opportunities for male and female inmates, women did not appear to succeed as well in academic and vocational training programs with men as they did in institutions with predominantly or exclusively female populations. Also, trying to manage a single institution that tried to serve both men and women created tremendous and unexpected administrative headaches for wardens.

By the 1990s, co-corrections was an experiment on the verge of abandonment. The Federal Bureau of Prisons had rejected co-corrections entirely, and fewer than thirty state co-correctional facilities remained in operation. Co-corrections did not seem to be a concept with significant prospects for revival.

Federal Bureau of Prisons

Federal Correctional Institution, Lexington, Kentucky.

Co-correctional industrial operations at the Federal Correctional Institution, Lexington, Kentucky, ca. 1975.

Federal Bureau of Prisons

Federal Bureau of Prisons Director Myrl Alexander (right) shows Senator Robert F. Byrd (D-W. Va.) a model of the Federal Bureau of Prisons institution then under development for Morgantown, West Virginia (ca.1967). The Morgantown facility was one of the first to implement functional unit management and Quay typology.

ALEXANDER'S BILL OF RIGHTS FOR INMATES

In 1956, corrections was still reeling from a series of riots, but was on the cusp of far-reaching Medical Model reforms. The President of the American Correctional Association during that year was Myrl E. Alexander (1909-1993), an Assistant Director of the Federal Bureau of Prisons who would later serve as its Director. In his presidential address, he enunciated "a bill of rights for the person under restraint in a free, democratic society" that echoed the National Prison Congress' Declaration of Principles of 1870, and anticipated the greater recognition of inmates' rights that would appear in the 1960s. That "Bill of Rights" included:

1. The *right* to clean, decent surroundings with competent attention to [the inmate's] physical and mental well-being

2. The *right* to maintain and reinforce the strengthening ties which bind [inmates] to [their] family and to [their] community

3. The *right* to develop and maintain skills as a productive worker in our economic system

4. The *right* to fair, impartial, and intelligent treatment without special privilege or license for any [inmate]

5. The *right* to positive guidance and counsel from correctional personnel possessed of understanding and skill

8

The Balanced Model

The 1960s were the high-water mark for prisoner rehabilitation philosophies. Idealistic objectives for prisons that were humane, constructive, and rehabilitative were set in prison policies and regulations throughout the United States, and administrators were making sincere efforts to realize those objectives in practice.

Then in the 1970s and 1980s, American corrections underwent an upheaval. Perhaps more than at any other point in their history, American prisons came under attack. Prisons were attacked by inmates and inmate rights groups, by scholars, by judges, and, most tellingly, by prison administrators themselves. The Medical Model was over.

By the 1970s, prison administrators were reaching out to achieve racial and sexual diversity among prison staff. Training program held at the New York City Department of Corrections.

New York City Department of Corrections

Not Everything Works

In 1974 and 1975, Robert Martinson published findings that suggested that treatment programs in New York State prisons had failed to reduce recidivism. A few years later, Martinson backed off somewhat from his initial implication that treatment programs were futile. Yet, he helped set off a national debate over what to do in light of his assertion that "nothing works."

Others took up the case against the Medical Model. Perhaps the most influential was University of Chicago Law School Dean Norval Morris. Medical Model programs, he argued, were coercive and cruel, and encouraged deceit. Prisoners were herded into treatment programs, whether or not they wanted to take them or were prepared to benefit from them. Indeterminate sentencing, a Medical Model staple that was geared toward rehabilitation and individualized treatment, merely created confusion and anxiety for inmates who could not predict when their sentences would end. Further, the system encouraged inmates to connive or play games in hopes of persuading prison or parole officials that they had seen the light and had become rehabilitated.

Norval Morris, the highly influential critic of the Medical Model and coercive rehabilitation methods.

Federal Bureau of Prisons

For Morris, the answer was not to discard the treatment programs, but, rather, to discard the theory behind them. What was needed was a more realistic appraisal of what programs could and could not accomplish, and an elimination of the Medical Model's coercive flavor—the subjective control over an inmate's life that was a product of defining the prison official as the physician, the inmate as the patient who needed to be cured, and the treatment program as the medicine.

Morris took the position that inmates had to have the proper personal motivation or commitment to benefit from educational, psychological, or other programs. Such programs could be very useful and should be offered to inmates in as normal and non-regimented a facility as possible, but, he assserted, program participation should not be mandatory. Furthermore, release from prison should be based on an objective schedule—not on the unreliable and subjective determinations provided for by indeterminate sentencing.

According to Federal Bureau of Prisons Director Norman A. Carlson, Morris gave intellectual respectability to what prison officials had already come to understand. In Carlson's view, Morris' point "was the same thing that many of us had thought for a number of years: that we in corrections could not coerce or force change. We could facilitate change, however, and we had that obligation as part of our responsibilities."

In 1975, the Federal Bureau of Prisons formally abandoned the Medical Model. In so doing, Carlson said, the Bureau was recognizing that nobody was powerful enough to diagnose and cure criminal behavior. Yet, Carlson emphasized that in abandoning the Medical Model, the Bureau was "not abandoning [its] efforts to assist inmates." On the contrary, by abandoning coercive rehabilitation, the Bureau was accepting the responsibility to "develop more and better programs" that would "interest inmates in helping themselves."

Norman A. Carlson, Director, Federal Bureau of Prisons 1970-1987 and American Correctional Association President 1979-1980.

American Correctional Association

The following year, the Bureau opened its first post-Medical Model facility: the Federal Correctional Institution in Butner, North Carolina. Based on Morris' principles, it featured an open, "normalized" environment, in which inmates were fairly free to move about within the secure perimeter during certain hours. It also offered a wide range of modern, innovative programs. However, apart from work assignments (which were mandatory, in part for purposes of inmate management), participation in those programs was voluntary. Butner attracted worldwide attention and was enormously influential.

Recognizing that rehabilitation could not be coerced was only one aspect of the dismantling of the Medical Model. The other was putting the goal of rehabilitation into a new perspective.

Under the Medical Model, rehabilitation clearly was enshrined as the paramount goal of prisons. In rejecting the Medical Model, the Federal Bureau of Prisons recognized that the other goals of imprisonment—punishment, deterrence, and incapacitation—were equally important. They reflected public demands and they protected public safety. Punishment, deterrence, and incapacitation joined rehabilitation as co-equal objectives. Because they were of equal importance or equal weight, they formed the "Balanced Model" of corrections. The Balanced Model became the blueprint for corrections from the 1970s to the present.

The barracks-style housing units at Lake County Correctional Facility, Tiptonville, Tennessee were representative of one style of prison housing in the 1970s and 1980s. Other examples of prison architecture and living conditions during those years are depicted on pages 199-211.

American Correctional Association

Reform and Retribution: An Illustrated History of American Prisons

California Department of Corrections

General population cellblock Deuel Vocational Institution, California (1976).

The Balanced Model

New prison construction in the 1970s and 1980s sometimes involved the addition of modern facilities to aging structures, as these three views of Trenton State Prison in New Jersey suggest.

The Gruzen Partnership/Grad Partnership, a joint venture–Michael Savoi, AIA partner-in-charge; Burton W. Berger, AIA project director

Design Space International (DSI) Company

Modular facilities at Philadelphia House of Corrections.

New administration building and housing units alongside old factory buildings and cellhouses at North Carolina Central Prison, Raleigh.

Hellmuth, Obata, and Kassabaum, Inc., Architects

The Western Missouri Correctional Center (Cameron, Missouri) and the Columbia Correctional Institution (Portage, Wisconsin) are based on designs that were highly common for medium-security facilites erected in the 1970s and 1980s. Decentralized housing units and open compounds frame factories and administration buildings.

Potter, Lawson, and Pawlowsky

Corrections Today

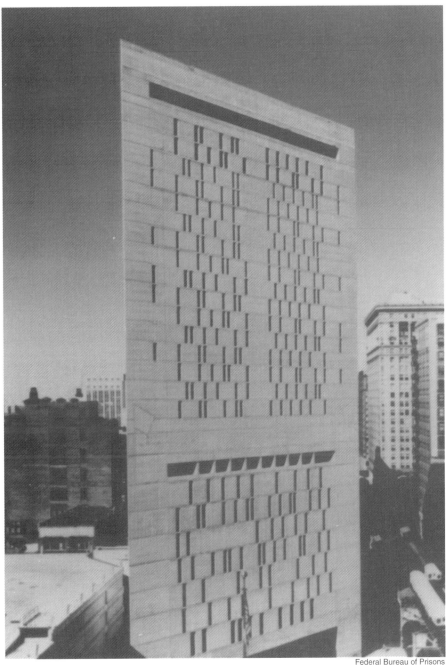

Federal Bureau of Prisons

The Federal Bureau of Prisons's Metropolitan Detention Center in Chicago, Illinois (opened in 1976) was typical of high-rise urban jail facilities built in the 1970s and 1980s. Established primarily to hold inmates awaiting trial or sentencing, these facilities were built near downtown courthouses and were designed to blend in with the urban surroundings.

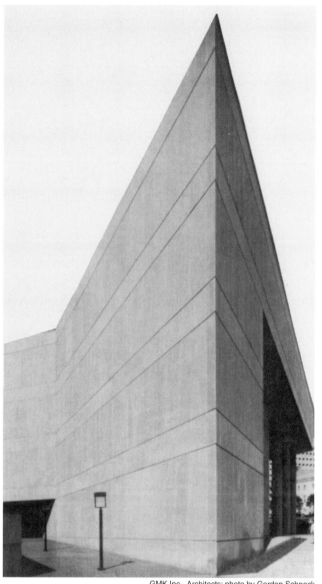

Richland County Judicial Center,
South Carolina.

GMK Inc., Architects; photo by Gordon Schneck

Montana State Prison.

Montana Department of Corrections

Reform and Retribution: An Illustrated History of American Prisons

Oahu Community Correctional Center, Honolulu, Hawaii.

Associated Architects and Engineers of Hawaii

Maryland Department of Corrections

Medium-Security Annex, Jessup, Maryland.

The Piedmont Correctional
Facility, North Carolina.

Henningson, Durham, and Richardson, Architects

South Carolina Department of Corrections

Women's Correctional Center, South Carolina.

Nevada Department of Corrections

Nevada State Prison.

The Durrant Group

Whiteside County Law Enforcement Center, Illinois.

Henningson, Durham, and Richardson, Architects; photo by David Wilson

Medium-Security Institution, Brunswick County, Virginia.

Hellmuth, Obata, and Kassabaum, Inc., Architects

Hiland Mountain Correctional Center,
Eagle River, Alaska.

Modern version of radial-style cellblocks, at the Marine Corps'
Correctional Facility, Camp Pendleton, California.

American Correctional Association

Michigan Department of Corrections

Housing units at Huron Valley Women's Prison, Michigan.

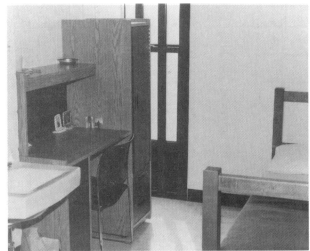

Federal Bureau of Prisons

Cell in medium-security federal prison, early 1980s.

Housing units built in the 1970s and 1980s, such as this one at the Trenton State Prison in New Jersey, featured common areas and cells that were easier to supervise from a single vantage point.

The Gruzen Partnership/Grad Partnership, a joint venture–Michael Savoi, AIA partner-in-charge; Burton W. Berger, AIA project director

Federal Bureau of Prisons

Housing Units built in the 1970s and 1980s typically featured common areas surrounded by two levels of cells as shown here at the Federal Correctional Institution, Phoenix.

Cell in Special Offender Center, State Maximum-Security Facility, Monroe, Washington, early 1980s. Televisions are sometimes placed in cells of inmates who are separated from the general population, partly to provide closed-circuit access to religious, educational, and other prison programs that such inmates are not permitted to attend in person.

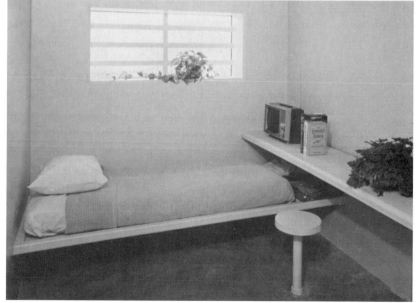

Walker McGough Foltz Lyerla, P.S., Architects

Wichita County Detention Center

Henningson, Durham, and Richardson, Architects

The Utah Regional Secure Facility in Draper and the Wichita County Detention Center in Wichita Falls, Texas followed the two-level tier design.

Riots and Resistance

The American political climate of the early 1960s that invested great faith in the government to solve social problems reinforced the Medical Model. The political culture of the late 1960s, with its strains of civil disobedience, nonnegotiable demands, anti-establishment confrontation, and violent rebellion, helped bring it down. As scholars and prison officials were striving to redefine the theoretical mission of imprisonment, inmates and inmate-rights activists were attacking imprisonment directly.

Nearly one hundred riots occurred in American prisons in 1969 and 1970 alone. Some were spontaneous and involved only a handful of inmates. Others involved large numbers of inmates who were seething over prison conditions and inspired by riots and demonstrations in American cities and on college campuses, and who were able to act deliberately and even with an unusual degree of solidarity.

Riots flared up during the late 1960s and early 1970s at Soledad Prison and San Quentin in California, the North Carolina Central Prison, and Holmsburg Prison in Philadelphia, among others. The violence continued into the 1980s, with major riots at Pennsylvania's Graterford Prison, the Michigan State Prison in Jackson, and at San Quentin. One of the most shocking disturbances was the bloody uprising at the New Mexico State Penitentiary in February 1980, where inmates killed and mutilated thirty-three fellow prisoners, tortured eight officers, and virtually demolished the prison.

Law enforcement personnel gather outside New Mexico State Penitentiary in Santa Fe during catastrophic uprising in February 1980.

Corrections Today, August 1988

Corrections Today, August 1988

Blood-spattered wall at New Mexico Penitentiary, photographed following 1980 riot.

Inmates trashed this cell at the Nevada State Prison during a riot in February 1978.

Washoe County (Nevada) Sheriff's Department

New York Department of Corrections

The maximum-security prison in Attica, New York, built in 1931, was the site of one of America's bloodiest prison riots in 1971.

New York state troopers on a cellhouse roof during the Attica riot.

New York State Police

Perhaps the most famous prison riot in American history, however, occurred in September 1971, at the Attica State Prison in western New York. Although New York's Commissioner of Corrections, Russell Oswald, was considered a humane and progressive prison administrator, Attica—an aging, Gothic, Auburn-style facility—was deficient in many ways. Inmates were frustrated over many of the usual concerns, such as poor food and inadequate health care. Most significant, however, was the cultural and racial gulf that separated the predominantly minority and urban inmates from the almost exclusively white and rural officers. The riot broke out after several years of escalating tension, and it was brought to a violent end in an armed assault on the prison by state police. The riot cost the lives of eleven correctional officers, who had been held hostage, and thirty-two inmates.

Hostage survivors identify dead inmates who had tried to protect them and other hostages.

New York State Police

New York State Police

Inmates hold knives to throats of hostages, minutes before police launch their assault on Attica, September 13, 1971.

Dead inmates after the assault on Attica.

New York State Police

Reform and Retribution: An Illustrated History of American Prisons

Attica became an emotion-charged symbol for inmates' rights activists, some of whom envisioned an end to the sanction of incarceration. The National Prison Project of the American Civil Liberties Union, the Soledad Brothers Defense Fund, and the American Friends Service Committee campaigned for improvements in prison conditions. The National Moratorium on Prison Construction attempted to block the erection of new prisons. Even the federally funded National Advisory Commission on Criminal Justice Standards and Goals urged a halt in prison expansion. Community-based sanctions were widely put forth as an across-the-board alternative to incarceration.

This machine shop at Huntsville State Prison in Texas, illustrates the conditions in which inmates sometimes lived and worked in the 1950s. By the 1960s and 1970s, inmates were able to challenge such conditions in the courts rather than by rioting.

Texas Department of Corrections

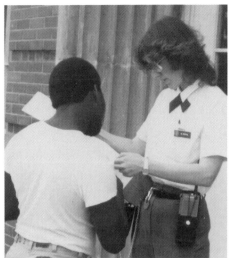

Federal Bureau of Prisons

A critically important advance in American prison administration during the 1970s and 1980s was the increasing diversity of staff—partly in an effort to counteract the racial tensions and misunderstandings between staff and inmates that had contributed to disturbances at Attica and elsewhere. By the 1970s, female correctional officers were being assigned to federal prisons that housed male inmates.

To some extent, inmate advocacy groups tried to discredit even those prison administrators, such as the Federal Bureau of Prisons' Norman Carlson, who endorsed change. But, it reasonably could be argued that Carlson—with his commitment to maintaining clean and humane prisons, his pivotal role in creating halfway houses, his willingness to introduce inmate grievance procedures, and his readiness to recruit minority staff and to work to diminish racial frictions—was vastly more effective at improving the lot of offenders than any of the inmate advocacy groups. The accomplishments of Carlson and those like him were all the more impressive in light of the American public's overwhelming hostility toward inmates and its complete lack of sympathy with the objectives of inmate advocacy groups.

On the other hand, the advocacy groups helped frame the debate over prisons in the 1970s and 1980s. Through individual and class action lawsuits that they filed on behalf of inmates, they helped stimulate a highly significant trend: the unprecedented intervention of the courts in corrections.

In 1971, Lee Jett (center) became the first African-American warden of a Federal Correctional Institution. He is at the Federal Correctional Institution at Englewood, Colorado. He is flanked by his associate wardens.

Federal Bureau of Prisons

ACA Accreditation

The setting of standards is an undertaking upon which most professions insist. Standards are especially important in the corrections profession, where public safety and the safety of both staff and inmates weigh in the balance.

Beginning in 1870, "the Declaration of Principles" adopted by the National Prison Congress provided a set of guidelines for corrections professionals to follow. In 1946, the American Prison Association published its first *Manual of Prison Standards*. In the 1960s, the American Correctional Association's Executive Secretary, E. Preston Sharp, and Colorado prison official C. Winston Tanksley, worked to develop a modern, comprehensive set of standards, and to build a system to obtain voluntary compliance with these standards through the accreditation of correctional institutions.

The work of Tanksley and Sharp culminated in 1974 with the creation of the American Correctional Association's Commission on Accreditation for Corrections (CAC). Under its first Director, Robert Fosen, the CAC began to distribute standards and accept applications from correctional facilities seeking accreditation. Accreditation would be granted or withheld based on appraisals of all aspects of a prison's operations: minimum space per inmate, health care services, diet, recreation, educational programs for inmates, training programs for staff, and so forth.

In 1978, the Commission on Accreditation for Corrections granted its first accreditations. By 1995, more than 1,400 correctional programs and institutions were accredited or seeking accreditation. Standards and accreditation, the great-grandchild of the 1870 "Declaration of Principles," continues to play a critical role in improving prison conditions and enhancing the professionalism of corrections staff.

Judicial Intervention

Before the 1960s, courts generally refused to exert much authority over prison conditions or operations. Little had changed since 1871, when, in *Ruffin v. Commonwealth* (62 Va. 790), the Supreme Court declared that prisoners were "slaves of the state," with no constitutional rights. As late as 1954, in *Banning v. Looney* (213 F.2d 771), a federal circuit court ruled that judges did not have "the power to supervise prison administration or to interfere with ordinary prison rules or regulations."

The civil rights movement of the 1960s helped galvanize inmates and such advocacy groups as the American Civil Liberties Union's National Prison Project to challenge prison conditions in court as violations of basic constitutional rights. Momentary public revulsion over Attica and the exposure of horrendous conditions in many prisons encouraged the trend.

In *Fulwood v. Clemmer* (206 F.Supp. 370 [1962]), a federal district court found that an inmate's isolation in solitary confinement for two years constituted cruel and unusual punishment, and hence was prohibited by the Constitution. In *Cooper v. Pate* (378 U.S. 546 [1964]), a case involving an Illinois state inmate's claims that prison officials had abridged his right to practice his religion, the Supreme Court established the principle that inmates retained constitutional rights and that they could sue to protect them. In 1974, the Supreme Court reasserted that position in *Wolff v. McDonnell* (418 U.S. 539), stating there was "no iron curtain drawn between the Constitution and the prisons of this country."

As inmate litigiousness increased, so did the importance of staff training which could help ensure more professional policies and procedures. Shown here are staff at the Federal Bureau of Prisons' Training Academy in Glynco, Georgia, in the late 1980s.

Federal Bureau of Prisons

Those decisions opened the floodgates to tens of thousands of individual and class action lawsuits. The litigation challenged virtually every aspect of prison operations, including housing, crowding, health care, diet, mail privileges, recreation, classification, and even the permissibility of inmates participating in artificial insemination programs. In many cases, courts found such deplorable conditions and practices to exist that they adopted various measures to correct them. Courts imposed population caps, issued orders mandating changes, appointed special masters to monitor conditions in prison systems under court orders and report on the level of compliance, and issued contempt citations when compliance was unsatisfactory. By 1982, prison systems in more than forty states were operating under court orders addressing crowding or conditions of confinement.

Probably the most significant conditions of confinement case was *Ruiz v. Estelle*, (503 F.Supp. 1265) in which the Fifth Federal Circuit Court ruled that substandard living conditions in Texas state prisons were unconstitutional. Severe crowding, the practice of allowing inmates to supervise other inmates, corporal punishment, and inadequate medical care were pervasive. The court ordered a complete restructuring of the Texas Department of Corrections and appointed a special master to ensure compliance. The case, first brought to the courts in 1974, was not settled until 1992.

Staff training class, Arlington (Virginia) Sheriff's Department, 1980s.

Capitol Communications

Not all of the lawsuits resulted in inmate victories. Frequently, courts ruled in favor of prison systems. The Supreme Court ruled in *Rhoades v. Chapman* (452 U.S. 337) that crowding was not unconstitutional, that single-bunking in cells was not required by the Constitution, and that "the Constitution does not mandate comfortable prisons." Similarly, in *Bell v. Wolfish*, (441 U.S. 520) the Supreme Court ruled that double-bunking and various security procedures such as body searches were constitutional in pretrial detention facilities. And in *Bono v. Saxbe* (620 F2d 609 [1979]) and *Bruscino v. Carlson*, (652 F.Supp. 609 [1988]), the Federal Seventh Circuit Court ruled that the high security operations at the U.S. Penitentiary at Marion, Illinois, were constitutional.

Court intervention was not inevitable. The Federal Bureau of Prisons was able to avoid the kind of judicial intervention that befell numerous state systems because its history of professional leadership (rather than rule by political appointees) had prevented the development of the sorts of objectionable conditions and practices that the courts targeted. The Bureau faced court challenges that sometimes led to modifications of specific conditions or practices. But, it did not experience the level of intense court supervision that occurred in some states, which included the control of prisons being relinquished to courts and operations being supervised by court-appointed special masters.

Firearms training for officers of the Federal Bureau of Prisons and the Florida Department of Corrrections (opposite page).

Federal Bureau of Prisons

Moreover, with Norman Carlson as Director during the period of greatest judicial activism, the Bureau was extremely responsive to the courts. According to Carlson, the Bureau "attempted to anticipate the direction in which the courts were moving and to modify its programs and operations accordingly." As a result, the Bureau "was not forced to become defensive and reactive after the courts intervened."

After judges complained informally to him about inadequate procedures for inmates to seek redress of grievances, for instance, Carlson moved quickly to implement a new grievance structure. He thereby averted judicial intervention and produced a grievance mechanism that many judges held up as a model for other systems to emulate.

By the mid-1990s, with public sentiment against inmates intensifying, campaigns were launched to curb inmate litigation and judicial intervention. Political and media attention focused on frivolous lawsuits filed by inmates to obtain certain varieties of peanut butter or brands of athletic shoes.

Nevertheless, judicial intervention had played an inestimable role in relieving inhumane and intolerable conditions, and even prison administrators lamented the prospect that courts might have to back away from providing oversight.

Florida Department of Corrections

Super-maximum Custody

A super-maximum custody prison is the most secure level of prison there is. Inmates are under stringent restrictions and supervision. Often, they are locked in their cells for up to twenty-three hours per day. Contact visits, where inmates actually touch visitors, may be prohibited. Physical contact with staff and other inmates is limited. Cells are constructed and furnished in such a way as to eliminate any kinds of materials that an inmate may use to fashion a weapon. The most advanced security equipment and procedures are used.

A minuscule number of inmates are held in super-maximum custody. For example, less than 1 percent of the Federal Bureau of Prisons' inmate population is housed in the Bureau's most secure facility, in Florence, Colorado. Yet super-maximum custody incarceration has been an important target of litigation, and the small number of inmates housed in such facilities has received a highly disproportionate amount of media and public attention.

Armed officer on tower duty at maximum-security prison.

American Correctional Association

Reform and Retribution: An Illustrated History of American Prisons

Arlington Department of Corrections

Shanks, picks, clubs, and other weapons confiscated from inmates underscore the need for high-security operations.

American Correctional Association

Double-perimeter fence with multiple rows of coiled razor wire.

One of the thorniest problems for prison administrators has always been finding appropriate ways to handle the most disruptive, volatile, assaultive, and predatory inmates, who pose immediate and extreme threats not only to staff but also to other inmates. Two basic methods have evolved for doing so: the dispersion model and the concentration model.

Under the dispersion model, the most dangerous inmates are scattered to high-security penitentiaries throughout a prison system, in hopes of diluting their impact. Prison systems that have tried the dispersion model, however, have found that it merely tends to spread problems from one location to many. Dangerous inmates are able to cause trouble, disrupt activities, and heighten tension at several institutions at once. That, in turn, affects procedures and resources at each of those institutions.

Federal Bureau of Prisons

Architectect's rendering of the Administrative Maximum-Security Penitentiary in Florence, Colorado, the Federal Bureau of Prisons' most secure facility.

Federal Bureau of Prisons

U.S. Penitentiary in Marion, Illinois, was the Federal Bureau of Prisons' super-maximum security facility in the 1970s and 1980s.

Correctional officer delivers meal to inmate in cell, United States Penitentiary at Marion, Illinois.

Federal Bureau of Prisons

(Bottom, left) Typical cell at the U.S. Penitentiary in Marion, Illinois, when it was a super-maximum facility. The plumbing fixtures, lighting fixtures, and furnishings were built to resist tampering by inmates who could fashion weapons out of ordinary fixtures and furnishings (note that the mattress that normally would be placed on the concrete slab is not shown).

Federal Bureau of Prisons

Federal Bureau of Prisons

(Above) Inmate law library at super-maximum penitentiary in Marion, Illinois. Only one person at a time was permitted to use the law library. Therefore, each unit had its own law library.

Federal Bureau of Prisons

Moving inmates to recreation yard at the United States Penitentiary at Marion, Illinois required one officer per each inmate as an escort.

The concentration model has proven much more successful. By placing all of a prison system's most dangerous inmates at one site, in highly controlled, super-maximum custody facilities, the ability of such inmates to spread mayhem is contained. Resources for handling problem cases can be focused on a single institution, and appropriate practices—such as extremely tight procedures for moving inmates from one part of the institution to another—can be adopted. The concentration model thereby frees up resources at other facilities, and enables those facilities to avoid having to follow special procedures for handling exceptionally predatory inmates. By the early 1990s, at least thirty-seven jurisdictions in the United States had adopted the concentration model, and approximately 13,000 inmates were housed in super-maximum custody institutions.

Another important benefit of the concentration model is that it gives prison administrators a valuable tool to preserve order in other prisons. Inmates in minimum-security camps know that disciplinary infractions can result in their transfer to medium-security institutions. Medium-security inmates know that disruptive behavior can land them in a maximum-security penitentiary. And for penitentiary inmates, knowing that they can be transferred to a super-maximum custody institution where they would be confined to their cells most of the day and lose access to some program opportunities is a powerful disincentive that can help maintain discipline.

From 1934 to 1963, the U.S. Penitentiary at Alcatraz, California, was the Federal Bureau of Prisons' super-maximum custody facility. Alcatraz was the country's prototype super-maximum prison, and the Bureau placed its most notorious and violent inmates there. In the 1960s and 1970s, however, following deactivation of Alcatraz, the Bureau experimented with the dispersion model. Violence in federal penitentiaries gradually escalated until the Bureau faced a crisis by the late 1970s and early 1980s.

Model of Minnesota Correctional Facility at Oak Park Heights, Minnesota's most secure prison.

Minnesota Department of Corrections

Assault rates declined not only at Marion, but throughout the system, and many wardens of the Federal Bureau of Prisons attributed the decline to the concentration of dangerous inmates under super-maximum custody.

Although the U.S. Penitentiary at Marion, Illinois, had been designed to replace Alcatraz, it was not used for that purpose at first. It operated as a regular penitentiary until 1983. In 1983, however, Marion was redesignated as a super-maximum facility in response to increasing violence at Marion and at other penitentiaries. The Bureau thus returned to the concentration model. Assault rates declined, not only at Marion but throughout the system, and many wardens in the Bureau attributed the decline to the reconcentration of dangerous inmates under super-maximum custody.

In the 1980s and 1990s, a new generation of super-maximum custody penitentiaries was built. The California Department of Corrections opened Pelican Bay; the Colorado system opened a super-maximum custody prison in Canon City; Oak Park Heights served as Minnesota's most secure facility; and the Federal Bureau of Prisons returned Marion to the status of a regular penitentiary and opened a new super-maximum facility in Florence, Colorado. Closed circuit television surveillance, computerized locking devices, and other high technology applications were introduced at the new prisons. Those innovations, as well as improved layouts of housing units, ensured tight security with fewer occasions to have to place inmates in handcuffs and other physical restraints. High technology and new designs also reduced occasions of physical contact between staff and inmates, thereby reducing chances for violence.

Control room for Special Offender Center at the Washington State Maximum-Security Facility in Monroe.

Walker McGough Foltz Lyerla, P.S., Architects

By maintaining good conduct, almost all of the inmates sent to Marion were able to return to less restrictive facilities.

Contrary to overwrought, highly dramatized criticism of super-maximum incarceration, there is not more violence in such facilities but far less; inmates are not subjected to sensory deprivation techniques, but have access to books, periodicals, art supplies, and television programs, can send and receive mail, can place telephone calls, are interviewed and counseled frequently by staff, and can meet with visitors. Further, inmates do not languish indefinitely in super-maximum prisons but typically spend only brief portions of their sentences in them. On average, for example, inmates spent about four years at Marion, while serving sentences that averaged forty years. By maintaining good conduct, almost all of the inmates sent to Marion were able to return to less restrictive facilities.

Super-maximum custody prisons have been the subject of lawsuits and bitter, inflammatory denunciations. Courts, however, as well as congressional inquiries, usually have found them to comply with constitutional safeguards. In some cases, they have required them to make modifications that brought them into compliance. In the 1990s, with an influx into prisons of gang members and other offenders with criminal histories of extreme violence, the need for super-maximum custody facilities seems greater than ever. In the view of prison administrators, the motivation is the most humane of all: super-maximum custody facilities save lives.

An American Correctional Association accreditation committee meeting in the early 1980s.

American Correctional Association

9

Seems Like Old Times

American Correctional Association (photo by Jay Aldrich of the *Gardnerville Record-Courier*)

Makin' little ones out of big ones. Inmates on the rock pile at Nevada State Prison in Carson City (1977). By the 1990s, assigning inmates to gravel-making enterprises had acquired considerable political cachet.

If there were ever a truism in corrections, it might be an observation made in 1955 by Federal Bureau of Prisons Director James V. Bennett: prisons "are as frequently accused of being too soft as they are of being too severe."

In the 1970s, in the wake of the Attica riot, prisons indeed were accused of being too severe. In the 1990s, with growing public frustration and resentment over crime, prisons were accused of being too soft. Neither accusation had the merit that accusers thought, but they put prison administrators on the defensive and affected prison operations.

Rhetoric from the 1970s about cold, punishment-obsessed administrators, cruel officers, browbeaten inmates, and horrendous living conditions, gave way by the 1990s to rhetoric about bleeding-heart, rehabilitation-obsessed administrators, weak officers, pampered inmates, and luxurious conditions.

Prisons in the mid-1990s, however, were hardly luxurious. With a higher rate of incarceration in the United States than in any other developed country, the inmate population was outpacing available bedspace. Double, triple, and quadruple-bunking was not out of the ordinary, nor was the placement of cots in corridors and other common areas—to the detriment not simply of prisoner comfort but also to the detriment of prison security.

Corrections Today, April 1986

Typical dormitory housing in the 1980s and 1990s was tightly packed and consisted of bunks, lockers, and perhaps waist-high partitions—hardly the vacation spots decried by indignant critics. Pictured (this page and lower right of facing page): Southern State Correctional Facility, Leesburg, New Jersey; Utah State Prison, Draper; Wyoming Correctional Facility, Attica, New York; Medium Security Prison, Orleans, New York.

Gelco Space

Other aspects of prison life, likewise, were at odds with the popular images of incarceration in the 1990s. In federal prisons, for example, inmates were fed three meals a day at a total cost of only about $2.60 per inmate per day—not much of a target for crusading reformers intent on rooting out excessive spending on inmates, but one that drew fire from partisans nonetheless. And inmates worked thirty-eight hours a week—in contrast with popular images of inmates lounging about on taxpayer-subsidized vacations.

Federal Bureau of Prisons

Cafeteria-style prison mess halls are efficient, inexpensive (less than $3.00 a day per inmate), and an important source of jobs, keeping inmates at work preparing food and busy on clean-up details.

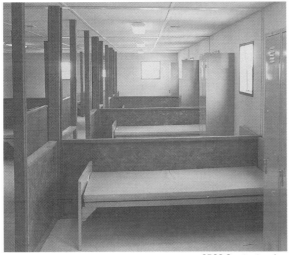

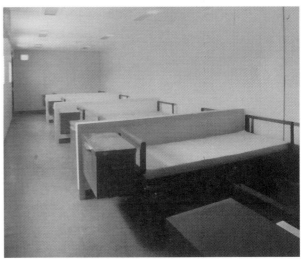

CRSS Constructors, Inc.

New York Department of Corrections

As for rehabilitation, meanwhile, prison administrators had settled that debate twenty years earlier—*against* rehabilitation (or, at least, coercive rehabilitation) as the primary goal of incarceration. Educational, recreational, and counseling programs were still being offered, but only partly to give inmates who wished to take advantage of them opportunities to change their lives and return to the community as law-abiding citizens. Just as important, such programs gave inmates easily supervised, well-structured activities for their nonwork hours, thereby relieving prison tensions and enhancing prison management. Still, opinion makers in the 1990s perpetuated the myth that the Medical Model still held sway.

National "get tough" attitudes on crime gave rise to a movement against fictitious prison luxuries. As a result, prison systems around the country were pressured to revive practices—such as chain gangs—that had been abandoned many decades before as impractical, unsafe, or inhumane. New York City even revived the nineteenth century expedient of incarcerating inmates on prison hulks.

Inmate industrial activities at Hennepin County Adult Detention Center, Minneapolis, Minnesota.

Hennepin County Sheriff's Department

Michigan Department of Corrections

Inmates in the State Prison of Southern Michigan relax in the yard during their nonworking hours, under conditions that are not nearly as festive as many members of the public imagine.

Austere cell at the Clark County Jail in Nevada.

A cell at the Stutsman County Jail in Jamestown, North Dakota, is decorated with a prisoner's family snapshots placed around the sheet of polished metal that serves as a mirror.

Nevada Department of Corrections

Corrections Today, December 1988

Privatization

In the nineteenth century, state governments unwilling to bear the expense of building and maintaining prisons solved the problem of punishing offenders by leasing them to private companies. The companies paid the state for the privilege of using inmates as forced labor, and assumed full responsibility for housing, feeding, and guarding them. The practice had largely disappeared by the 1890s.

A century later, however, an updated version of the idea was gaining momentum. Public demands to mete out longer sentences to criminals, a resulting shortage of prison bedspace, government belt-tightening, a readiness to try apparently cheap alternatives to traditional ways of carrying out public responsibilities, and fashionably cynical attitudes toward public service, helped create an environment favorable to privately owned, profit-making prisons.

Privately owned facilities had long been the norm in community corrections. Federal and state corrections agencies contracted with private vendors to hold the vast majority of halfway house inmates. A significant number of those privately owned halfway houses, however, were owned by not-for-profit organizations.

Control Center in Shelby Training Facility, operated by the Corrections Corporation of America.

Corrections Corporation of America

Florida Department of Corrections

Cellblock in a Florida state prison.

By the mid-1980s and into the 1990s, private corrections firms such as the Corrections Corporation of America, Wackenhut, Pricor, Buckingham, and the United States Corrections Corporation were expanding into the operation of secure facilities. State and county governments in California, Texas, Tennessee, Kentucky, New Mexico, Pennsylvania, and elsewhere, contracted with private companies to run jails, detention centers, and even low- and medium-security prisons. The federal government also contracted with private vendors to operate certain secure facilities, such as detention centers for the Immigration and Naturalization Service.

Various contractual arrangements emerged. In many cases, private corrections enterprises built and staffed their own facilities and signed contracts to provide bedspace in them for state or county offenders. Sometimes, however, private companies would simply move into government-built and owned prisons, and sign contracts to staff and manage them. For the public and the government, such arrangements offered a seemingly more cost-efficient quick fix to the puzzle of finding enough room for the burgeoning prison population. For the private corrections entrepreneurs, they offered access to a lucrative growth industry.

Serious questions persisted about the concept of privately run secure facilities, even as those facilities multiplied in the 1990s. Could they really do the job? Could they provide adequate security? Could they deliver necessary programs? Would they be accountable? Would they be liable for damages if problems occurred, or would the government be liable? What would happen if privately employed prison officers were allowed to go out on strike, unlike publicly employed officers? Despite some riots at privately owned detention facilities in the 1990s, prompted at least in part by inmate anger over poor food and substandard conditions, there was a growing consensus in the field by the mid-1990s that private corrections was maturing and demonstrating its competence. However, an even larger question continued to loom: were promises of cost savings being met? Some critics of private corrections cautioned that the cost savings might be illusory, especially as personnel costs escalated after the first few years of a contract, due to employees gaining seniority and higher pay. In 1996, in fact, a study undertaken by the U. S. General Accounting Office failed to discern any clear evidence that privatization of state prison operations actually cut costs at all.

Beyond the practical questions, there was a powerful philosophical one. In a democracy, the government has no greater power over its citizens than the power to incarcerate them. Criminal justice is a core activity of government, and incarceration is an intrinsic part of that function. Critics of corrections-for-profit have been skeptical about the propriety of allowing governments to put such a grave responsibility up for bid.

Back to Stripes

For centuries, prison reformers devoted themselves to improving prison conditions. In the 1990s, a new generation of prison reformers devoted themselves to making them worse. Capitalizing on erroneous public impressions that inmates were living the Life of Riley in resort-like surroundings, certain political figures campaigned to apply a little more sting to prison sentences.

Even the least restrictive prison is a prison. Even a minimum-security inmate is deprived of freedom, denied privacy, separated from loved ones, and required to follow orders dictating every aspect of his or her life: when to get up, what clothes to wear, what work to do, and even what to eat.

Diversions from the monotony of prison life are few and modest, and serve sound correctional purposes. After laboring for a full work week in prison factories or other prison jobs, inmates in most institutions are permitted to participate in self-improvement activities (Alcoholics Anonymous meetings, classes to improve job skills, arts and crafts, and so on). They can play soccer, handball, softball, or other sports; read books and periodicals in the institution library; meet visitors, if they are lucky enough to have any; and watch television—usually in large common areas, where program selections are made in advance to avoid disputes over what station to watch (cable access, where available, usually is paid for by the inmates themselves).

Religious service at a Colorado state prison.

Lieutenant Elmer Ahart, Colorado Correctional Facility, Canon City, Colorado

Such programs enable inmates to work off aggression, blow off steam, learn how to use leisure time in socially acceptable ways, and otherwise make it through ten or twenty grinding years of incarceration. These programs help reduce prison tension, which can be explosive—and quelling explosions is vastly more expensive than preventing them. Finally, it is easier, safer, and less costly to manage inmates who participate in structured activities. A patch of open space on the prison yard and a ball can keep twenty-two inmates out of trouble for an hour playing soccer—and afterwards, they will be sufficiently worn out so that they will be less likely to take a poke at an officer or at another inmate. Even palatable and reasonably varied food—albeit at less that $3.00 per day—can reduce the frustrations of being caged and thereby help prevent misbehavior.

Such prison activities are not costly, and they have very pragmatic goals. In the long run, they can make prisons less expensive by making them safer and easier to manage. They are the most effective way that outnumbered prison staff can control inmates.

Despite the limited scope, cost effectiveness, and pragmatism of programs, they became a convenient political target during an era when the electorate was increasingly sour and vaguely dissatisfied with most aspects of public policy. State and federal legislation in the 1990s was proposed—and in some cases passed—to make prisons even grimmer than they already were. Television would be limited to certain types of programming or eliminated entirely;

Visiting hours at a California state prison. Inmates who maintain strong family ties while incarcerated are better able to readjust to the community after release from prison.

California Department of Corrections

Reform and Retribution: An Illustrated History of American Prisons

Vocational training at the Maryland Correctional Institution in Jessup.

Stephen Steurer

weightlifting and certain other types of athletics would be prohibited; no musical instruments would be allowed; and there was even at least one attempt to legislate the types of meals that could be served. There were also calls to increase the typical inmate work week from forty hours to sixty hours—but no realistic suggestions about how to do so without inflicting damage upon the private sector.

Paradoxically, some of the "get tough" measures that were intended to impress the public actually may have imperiled public safety. In one southwestern state, a county sheriff stepped into the international limelight by placing inmates in tents—even though inmates can be monitored and secured much more effectively in traditional housing units and cellblocks than they can be in Andersonville-style tent prisons. And in several southeastern states, chain gangs began reappearing. A much reviled national embarrassment of the early twentieth century, chain gangs had great symbolic value in the 1990s, but little correctional value. They contributed nothing to public safety, because inmates behind prison walls clearly were less threatening to law-abiding citizens than those working along the sides of public thoroughfares, guarded by a few carbine-toting deputies.

Of course, public safety was not the point of such undertakings. Rather, the point was to create a public spectacle by degrading inmates. Possibly the most meaningful of the spectacles, however, was the decision, in several jurisdictions in the 1990s, to put inmates back in stripes.

The use of distinctive uniforms had dated back to the beginnings of the penitentiary system, when inmates at the Walnut Street Jail wore brightly colored uniforms when they worked outside the prison. Stripes came into general use in Auburn-style prisons of the nineteenth century, partly to identify inmates but also to emphasize the rigid control that was characteristic of Auburn-style institutions. Elmira-style reformatories began moving away from striped uniforms in the late nineteenth century, as part of their efforts to treat inmates with more dignity. Prisoners at the early federal penitentiaries at Leavenworth, Atlanta, and McNeil Island wore stripes in the 1890s, but after the turn of the century, striped uniforms were replaced by ordinary work clothes that were discreetly color-coded to identify the inmate's grade or classification. Stripes had largely vanished from American prisons by the 1930s, although they remained in some southern prisons until the 1960s.

Portsmouth, Virginia, Sheriff's Office

Reform and Retribution: An Illustrated History of American Prisons

Proponents of the return to chain gangs and stripes frankly admitted that the purpose of such innovations was to humiliate the inmates. According to the Sheriff of Marshall County, Alabama, "If we embarrass them enough by having to wear these old-time chain gang black and whites, maybe, just maybe, these guys will decide to stay out of here."

Merely depriving inmates of their liberties, in other words, was no longer enough. Before the eighteenth century, prisons held offenders awaiting punishment, but imprisonment itself was not considered punishment. From the 1800s on, however, prison *was* the punishment. Hence the expression, attributed to a British parole official of the 1930s, that individuals were sent to prisons "*as* punishment, not *for* punishment." In some jurisdictions, that principle was no longer entirely accepted in the 1990s.

Arlington, Virginia, Sheriff's Department

(Left and above) Inmate work crews on clean-up details along roads in Virginia, late 1980s.

Capital Punishment

In Colonial America, execution was the prescribed penalty for a host of crimes. By the late eighteenth century, as the United States moved toward imprisonment as the punishment for most crimes, the death penalty was reserved mainly for such offenses as murder, rape, treason, and espionage.

Since colonial times, well over 15,000 individuals have been legally executed, including more than 4,000 since 1930. A respite in carrying out executions in the United States occurred between 1972 and 1977, in light of the Supreme Court's ruling in *Furman v. Georgia* (408 U.S. 238) that the death penalty was administered in such a way as to constitute cruel and unusual punishment. The decision voided the federal death penalty and the death penalty in thirty-five states.

States quickly redrafted statutes to meet objections laid out in *Furman v. Georgia*. In *Gregg v. Georgia* (428 U.S. 153) and other cases in 1977, the Supreme Court found that several states had developed death penalty statutes that met constitutional requirements. Capital punishment resumed in January 1977, with Utah's execution of murderer Gary Gilmore.

Since the reintroduction of capital punishment, thirty-six states and the federal government have enacted death penalty statutes. Many of those jurisdictions, however, have yet to carry out an execution. Just three states—Texas, Florida, and Louisiana—have carried out most of the 200 or so executions since 1977.

Academic studies have questioned the death penalty on the grounds that no deterrent value can be established and because there may be patterns of racial discrimination in its application. Public sentiment, however, is overwhelmingly in favor of capital punishment. Reflecting that popularity, as well as rising public anger over convicted murderers drawing appeals out for many years on seemingly flimsy pretexts, legislative efforts were underway in the 1990s to limit court appeals of death sentences.

Executions often are not the responsibility of prison systems. The county prosecutor's office may have technical custody of the condemned inmate, rather than the state prison where that inmate is housed. And, prior to *Furman v. Georgia*, federal executions were carried out under the authority of U. S. Marshals, rather than the Federal Bureau of Prisons.

Prisons, however, obviously have a role to play in capital cases. Usually, they provide the site for carrying out an execution—most gallows, electric chairs, firing ranges, and gas chambers have been located behind prison walls. More recently, prisons in death penalty jurisdictions have installed lethal injection chambers. First proposed in the 1880s, lethal injections were not used in the United States until 1982, when the State of Texas adopted the procedure.

In addition, prison systems in death penalty jurisdictions frequently maintain a death row or special housing unit for those awaiting execution at selected maximum-security penitentiaries. Condemned inmates usually are identified as high-risk inmates—for escapes, violence, and suicide—and therefore may be separated from the general prison population. That is especially true for inmates nearing their execution dates. Special arrangements must be made to try to ensure that death row inmates have access to legal materials, opportunities to see visitors, and access to programs similar to those available to general population inmates.

Lethal injection chamber.

Federal Bureau of Prison

American Corrections Moves into the Twenty-first Century

More than one million Americans were behind bars in 1995. Although a leveling off of the prison population was projected by the turn of the century, some criminologists and demographers predicted a new expansion of the prison population early in the twenty-first century as the outcome of a tremendous increase in the number of people in the high-crime, high-violence, eighteen-to thirty-five-year-old age group at that time. Given such concerns, prisons in the 1990s already were formulating strategies for dealing with prospects for the 2000s.

An important design innovation, adopted by the Federal Bureau of Prisons and some state systems, was the development of correctional complexes. These complexes clustered several prisons together. Each prison would operate independently, with its own warden, its own staff, and its own mission. A single complex, for example, might include a minimum-security camp, a medium-security facility, and a maximum-security penitentiary.

Control room for the Piedmont Correctional Facility in North Carolina permits staff to control sally ports, observe activities, and respond to incidents throughout the institution.

Henningson, Durham, and Richardson, Architects

Prisons clustered in a complex could share services, such as power plants, personnel offices, procurement operations, and record-keeping, thus reducing costs. Transportation expenses could also be cut, as inmates requiring transfer to a different security level could be moved across the street, instead of hundreds of miles away. And, in the event of a disturbance or other problem at one of the institutions in the complex, staff at the neighboring institutions could provide immediate backup.

Prison systems also are applying impressive new technological advances to solve a number of problems. Retina imaging, iris scanning, and hand-geography will be faster and more reliable for inmate identification than fingerprinting; and bar-coded wristbands, access cards with magnetic data strips, electronic bracelets, and enhanced use of video cameras not only will ensure faster identification of inmates, staff, and visitors, but also will permit the control, tracking, and recording of their movements within the institution.

Warden Charles L. Ryan

Aerial view of the Arizona State Prison Complex in Florence, Arizona (opened 1991), which clustered several correctional facilities of various security levels.

Federal Bureau of Prisons

The Federal Prison Camp at Montgomery, Alabama, began operations in 1930 in the cluster of wooden barracks in the upper center of this photo; eventually, the barracks were surrounded by modern living units, factory buildings, and other structures. Federal Prison Camps first appeared on military bases in the 1930s. Frequently, inmates could be employed on cleanup and maintenance projects on the base, thereby freeing military personnel for other duties.

With the end of the Cold War and the onset of military downsizing in the 1980s and 1990s, there were increased opportunities to place low-security federal prisons on military bases. In 1988, this Federal Prison Camp was established in barracks at the Homestead Air Force Base in Florida.

Federal Bureau of Prisons

Security is already being enhanced by the use of tamper-resistant, electro-magnetic locking devices, vastly improved X-ray technology for detecting contraband, thermal-imaging eyewear for helping to observe inmates in low-light circumstances, video motion detector systems for alerting staff to persons in unauthorized areas, and ultrasound, rapid eye scans, vital signs monitoring bracelets, and air sampling equipment for detecting the presence of drugs. Nonlethal weapons, from stun guns and stun belts to variable threat lasers, also are being perfected. And to thwart airborne escapes, many prisons have strung cables between high poles, criss-crossing prison yards, to prevent helicopter landings.

Motion detection device attached to razor wire.

ACI Corporation

Control center for a single housing unit in a New York City correctional facility.

New York City Department of Corrections (Spencer Burnett)

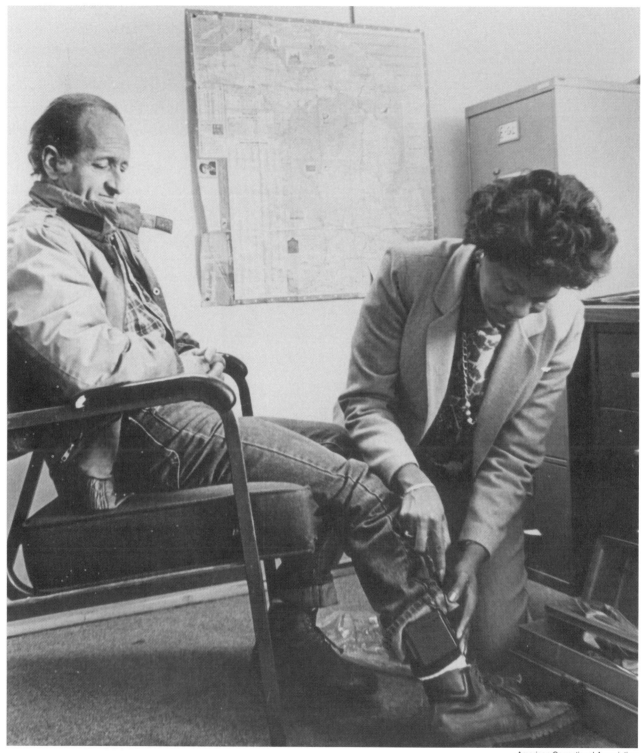

American Correctional Association

Parolee is fitted with electronic monitoring ankle bracelet.

Improved information technologies also are enhancing prison management. Information transmitted via Wide Area Networks (WANs) is helping to monitor gang activities in individual prisons as well as across entire prison systems. WANs also are making it easier and quicker to collect data, discern patterns in inmate behavior and institutional climates, and transmit orders, policy changes, inmate records, requests for information, and reports.

Other new technologies that have been implemented in many American prisons, or are likely to be, include telemedicine capability, which will reduce the need to transport inmates to community hospitals for treatment, video conferencing for use in parole hearings and arraignments, voice analysis identification (or "voice printing"), and improved body armor.

Even as the public turned its back on many types of rehabilitation programs for inmates in the 1990s, two types of prison programs continued to enjoy considerable support: work programs and drug treatment programs.

Work programs, particularly those involved in industrial production, have always had multiple and somewhat incompatible objectives: providing labor-intensive assignments as a prison management tool, to keep as many inmates as busy as possible; providing vocational training for inmates; making operations as efficient as possible to meet customer needs, while retaining inherently inefficient, labor-intensive procedures and deliberately restricting competitiveness to avoid hurting the private sector. Members of the public want inmates to work, but they do not want inmates to take away their own jobs.

Within those constraints, prison administrators must constantly monitor and revise work programs and vocational training programs to respond to changing times and new demands. Farming operations, once a major part of virtually every prison work program, were phased out most places in the 1970s when it became cheaper for prisons to purchase food from wholesale suppliers than to produce their own. Industrial product lines changed as customer needs changed: military supplies during World War II; reconditioning of office machines during the period of government retrenchment in the 1950s; data processing in the 1960s; ergonomic furniture, computer work stations, and office systems furniture in the 1970s and 1980s. Vocational training programs also had to be updated, with aviation mechanics during World War II, air conditioning and television repair being introduced in the 1950s, and computer training by the 1970s.

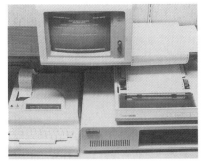

Contrar Controlled Activities Corporation

Electronic Monitoring Central Station.

Shock Incarcaration

One of the most celebrated prison initiatives of the 1980s and 1990s was "shock incarceration." Shock incarceration centers—also known as intensive confinement centers or boot camps—were established in many jurisdictions to put offenders through comparatively brief, military-style training programs as an alternative to longer sentences in traditional correctional facilities.

The earliest examples of such programs included the shock incarceration network inaugurated in New York state prisons in 1979, and the boot camps opened by the state corrections systems of Oklahoma and Georgia in 1983. By the mid-1990s, the Federal Bureau of Prisons and nearly three dozen state and county prison systems had established one or more boot camps. Although programs and requirements varied from system to system, boot camp placement typically was reserved for younger, nonviolent, first-time offenders. The idea was to "shock" those offenders at an early age, and mold their characters, so that they would not develop into career criminals. The earliest boot camps were exclusively for male offenders, but eventually many jurisdictions established boot camps for female offenders, as well. The period of incarceration in a boot camp generally ranged from three- to six-months, which, in many jurisdictions, was followed by a period of supervised release in the community.

New York Department of Corrections

Lakeview Shock Incarceration Facility, Brocton, New York.

New York Department of Corrections

Lakeview Shock Incarceration Facility, Brocton, New York.

Boot camp programs were extremely strenuous and rigidly structured. Military drills were a prominent feature, much as they were in Zebulon Brockway's reformatory program at Elmira (see Chapter 4). Physical training also was emphasized, such as calisthenics and hiking. Many boot camps also included hard physical labor, with squads assigned to such community service projects as preserving forests, repairing public buildings, constructing public recreational facilities, painting churches, and maintaining community parks and gardens. Some boot camp programs had instructional and counseling components, with rigorous academic classes, life skills training, and substance-abuse treatment. Drilling, physical training, work, and instruction generally filled virtually every moment of long, sixteen-hour days, permitting little or no leisure time for the inmates between reveille and taps.

Strict military discipline and spartan military living conditions were also a common feature of boot camps, with military uniforms and titles used in many of the programs, and inmates organized into platoons. Inmates were housed in barracks, were required to salute, and to address correctional officers as "sir" or "ma'am," and, in some jurisdictions, were subject to such summary punishments as having to do pushups or run laps, in addition to being verbally berated. Although subjecting boot camp inmates to summary punishments and yelling were popular with the public, they also were controversial, and many jurisdictions prohibited them.

Boot camps were one of the few alternative sanctions in the 1980s and 1990s that enjoyed broad support among elected officials and the public—mainly because they gave the appearance of being tough on criminals, and because it was presumed that intense military training methods could restructure the character of young offenders in beneficial ways. Boot camps had the added benefit of diverting inmates from more expensive bedspace in traditional prisons, thus containing costs and relieving crowding.

New York Department of Corrections
Lakeview Shock Incarceration Facility, Brocton, New York.

With the boot camp concept well into its second decade, however, research was unable to muster conclusive evidence that it was having much of an impact on recidivism. Some prison systems considered their intensive confinement experiments to be a success, such as New York's shock incarceration network, Oregon's SUMMIT program ("Success Using Motivation, Morale, Intensity, and Treatment"), and Vermont's program, which emphasized community service programs rather than military training ("the boot camp without the boot"). On the other hand, at least one state prison system—Arizona's—abandoned its boot camp program, explaining that it simply was not working, and pointing out that the recidivism rate for boot camp graduates was higher than that for inmates released from traditional prisons.

New York Department of Corrections

Lakeview Shock Incarceration Facility, Brocton, New York. Boot camps—also known as shock therapy centers or intensive confinement centers—emerged in the late 1980s as a highly disciplined, rigidly structured prison alternative for younger, first-time offenders.

To prepare for the twenty-first century, prison administrators in the 1990s were developing new initiatives that would ensure that the number of inmate jobs would keep pace with the number of inmates. Strategies being considered in various prison systems included recycling projects, sales to charitable and relief organizations, development of partnerships to manufacture and market certain products in conjunction with privately owned companies, and privatization of prison industrial programs.

Drug treatment was another program area receiving significant attention in the 1990s. Enactment of new drug laws and more vigorous prosecution of drug-related offenses led to a drastic increase in the number of federal and state inmates with histories of drug abuse. Prison systems responded by developing drug treatment programs.

In state prisons, participation in drug treatment programs rose from 4 percent of the inmate population in 1979 to over 13 percent by 1991. The Federal Bureau of Prisons, meanwhile, developed a model drug treatment program, in partnership with the National Institute on Drug Abuse. It featured a wide range of treatment options, including drug awareness education, residential treatment in special living units for inmates with severe drug abuse histories who were in the last months of their sentences, aftercare for inmates in residential programs who returned to the prison's general population, and aftercare in the community following release.

San Diego Sheriff's Department

Counselor meets with inmate to assess the inmate's need for substance-abuse programming.

So-called "special needs offenders" made up another segment of the inmate population requiring more attention from prison administrators as the twenty-first century dawned. Although young males continued to make up the largest component by far of the inmate population, as it always had, increasing numbers of female inmates, aging inmates serving life sentences, and even physically disabled inmates, compelled prison administrators to designate appropriate housing for them, to arrange for specialized health care, and to develop customized programs to ensure that special needs inmates would have parity with the majority of inmates.

Perhaps the most puzzling challenge for prison administrators of the twenty-first century, however, is likely to be trying to maintain sound prison operations in the face of a public that is indifferent or hostile. The public schizophrenia on prison issues has long troubled corrections professionals. The public is indignant when prisons appear too comfortable and horrified when riots such as the one at Attica demonstrate that they are not. It expects magical transformations in a criminal's behavior to occur during incarceration, yet are contemptuous of rehabilitation. Most of all, however, the public tends not to care. Prisoners are to be locked away and forgotten.

Prison staff, obviously, cannot forget inmates; they must work with them every day. Yet, unlike virtually every other public undertaking, prisons have no real constituency to provide support and foster understanding. Nevertheless, creating such understanding is vital. With public support and understanding, administrators can manage safe and humane prisons that protect society, punish and deter crime, incapacitate criminals, and provide opportunities for inmates to reform themselves.

Florida state correctional officers gather for commemoration of National Correctional Officers Week, in the mid-1980s.

Florida Department of Corrections

For Further Reading

Adamson, Christopher R. October 1983. "The Breakdown of Canadian Prison Administration: Evidence from Three Commissions of Inquiry." *Canadian Journal of Criminology*. 25: 433-446.

American Correctional Association. 1996. *Juvenile and Adult Boot Camps*. Lanham, Md.: American Correctional Association.

American Friends Service Committee. 1971. *Stuggle for Justice*. New York: Hill and Wang.

Barnes, Harry Elmer. 1944. *Report on the Progress of the State Prison War Program*. Washington, D.C.: War Production Board.

Barnes, Harry Elmer, and Negley K. Teeters. 1943. *New Horizons in Criminology: The American Crime Problem*. New York: Prentice-Hall.

Barry, John Vincent. 1958. *Alexander Maconochie of Norfolk Island*. Melbourne, Australia: Oxford University Press.

Bates, Sanford. 1971 reprint of 1936 original. *Prisons and Beyond*. Freeport, N.Y.: Books for Libraries Press.

Bennett, James V. 1970. *I Chose Prison*. New York: Alfred A. Knopf.

Binny, John, and Henry Mayhew. 1968 reprint of 1862 original. *The Criminal Prisons of London and Scenes of Prison Life*. New York: Reprints of Economic Classics.

Brockway, Zebulon R. 1968 reprint of 1912 original. *Fifty Years of Prison Service: An Autobiography*. Montclair, N.J.: Patterson Smith.

Brown, Dorothy M. 1984. *Mabel Walker Willebrandt: A Study in Power, Loyalty, and Law*. Knoxville: University of Tennessee Press.

Campbell, Charles. 1993. *The Intolerable Hulks: British Shipboard Confinement, 1776-1857*. Bowie, Md.: Heritage Books.

Carlson, Norman A. Spring 1976. "Corrections in the United States Today: A Balance Has Been Struck." *American Criminal Law Review*. 13: 615-647.

DiIulio, John J. 1987. *Governing Prisons: A Comparative Study of Correctional Management*. New York: Free Press.

Federal Bureau of Prisons. 1949. *Handbook of Correctional Institution Design and Construction*. Washington, D.C.: Federal Bureau of Prisons.

Foucault, Michel. 1977. *Discipline and Punish: The Birth of the Prison*. New York: Pantheon.

Holt, Raymond and Richard Phillips. Spring 1991. "Marion: Separating Fact from Fiction." *Federal Prisons Journal*. 2: 28-36.

Howard, D. C. 1958. *John Howard: Prison Reformer*. New York: Archer House.

Johnston, James A. 1949. *Alcatraz Island and the Men Who Live There*. New York: Charles Scribner's Sons.

Johnston, Norman. 1994. *Eastern State Penitentiary: A Crucible of Good Intentions*. Philadelphia: Philadelphia Museum of Art.

__. 1973. *The Human Cage: A Brief History of Prison Architecture*. Philadelphia: The American Foundation, Inc.

Kent, John. 1962. *Elizabeth Fry*. London: B.T. Batford, Ltd.

Keve, Paul W. 1981. *Corrections*. New York: John Wiley and Sons, Inc.

__. 1991. *Prisons and the American Conscience: A History of U.S. Federal Corrections*. Carbondale: Southern Illinois University Press.

Lewis, Orlando F. 1967 reprint edition. *The Development of American Prison Customs, 1776-1845*. Montclair, N.J.: Patterson Smith.

Lewis, W. David. 1965. *From Newgate to Dannemora: The Rise of the Penitentiary in New York, 1796-1848*. Ithaca, N.Y.: Cornell University Press.

Logan, Charles H. 1990. *Private Prisons: Cons and Pros*. New York: Oxford University Press.

McGrath, W. T. 1965. *Crime and its Treatment in Canada*. Toronto: MacMillan of Canada.

McKelvey, Blake. 1977 reprint edition. *American Prisons: A History of Good Intentions*. Montclair, N.J.: Patterson Smith.

McShane, Marilyn D. and Frank P. Williams III, eds. 1996. *Encyclopedia of American Prisons*. New York: Garland Publishers.

Morris, Norval. 1974. *The Future of Imprisonment*. Chicago: University of Illinois Press.

Morris, Norval and David J. Rothman, eds. 1995. *The Oxford History of the Prison: The Practice of Punishment in Western Society*. New York: Oxford University Press.

Oswald, Russell. 1972. *Attica—My Story*. Garden City, N.Y.: Doubleday & Co.

Pisciotta, Alexander. 1994. *Benevolent Repression: Social Control and the American Reformatory Movement*. New York: New York University Press.

Roberts, John W. 1994. *Escaping Prison Myths: Selected Topics in the History of Federal Corrections*. Washington, D.C.: American University Press.

Rothman, David J. 1971. *The Discovery of the Asylum: Social Order and Disorder in the New Republic*. Boston: Little, Brown.

Styles, Scott. Summer 1991. "Conditions of Confinement Suits." *Federal Prisons Journal*. 2: 41-7.

Sullivan, Larry E. 1990. *The Prison Reform Movement: Forelorn Hope*. Boston: Twayne Publishers.

Toch, Hans. Winter 1992. "Functional Unit Management: An Unsung Achievement." *Federal Prisons Journal*. 2: 15-9.

Vantour, Jim, ed. 1991. *Our Story: Organizational Renewal in Federal Corrections*. Ottawa: Correctional Service of Canada.

Wicker, Tom. 1975. *A Time to Die*. New York: Ballantine Books.

Index

About the Author

John W. Roberts is Chief of Communications and Archives for the Federal Bureau of Prisons in Washington, D.C. He holds a Ph.D. in history from the University of Maryland. His previous publications include *Escaping Prison Myths: Selected Topics in the History of Federal Corrections* (1994) and *Putting Foreign Policy to Work: The Role of Organized Labor in American Foreign Relations* (1995).

The opinions expressed in this book are those of the author and do not necessarily represent the positions of the Federal Bureau of Prisons, the United States Department of Justice, or the American Correctional Association.

S 090227